MW01698525

FEDERALISM

The Legacy of George Mason

GEORGE MASON

Painted in 1811 by D. W. Boudet, after a lost portrait by John Hesselius.

(Courtesy of the Virginia Museum, Richmond.)

THE GEORGE MASON LECTURES

FEDERALISM

The Legacy of George Mason

EDITED BY
MARTIN B. COHEN

George Mason
University Press
Fairfax, Virginia

Copyright © 1988 by
George Mason University Press

4400 University Drive
Fairfax, VA 22030

All rights reserved

Printed in the United States of America

British Cataloging in Publication Information Available

Distributed by arrangement with
University Publishing Associates, Inc.

4720 Boston Way
Lanham, MD 20706

3 Henrietta Street
London WC2E 8LU England

Library of Congress Cataloging-in-Publication Data

Federalism : the legacy of George Mason / edited by Martin B. Cohen.
p. cm. — (The George Mason Lectures ; 4)
Includes index.
ISBN 0-913969-10-9 (alk. paper)
ISBN 0-913969-11-7 (pbk. alk. paper)
1. Federal government—United States. 2. Federal government—Canada.
3. Mason, George 1725-1792. I. Cohen, Martin B., 1937- . II. Series.
KF4600.F43 1988
342.73'040—dc19
[347.30242] 87-32431 CIP

All George Mason University Press books are produced on acid-free paper which exceeds the minimum standards set by the National Historical Publications and Records Commission.

Contents

Introduction

While speaking in support of the Virginia Plan at the Constitutional Convention, Edmund Randolph is reported to have said, "The true question is whether we shall adhere to the federal plan, or introduce the national plan."[1] As far as William Paterson of New Jersey was concerned, the question had already been answered. "The idea of a national Govt as contradistinguished from a federal one, never entered into the mind of any of [the states]."[2] That some uncertainty existed regarding the meaning of "federal" seems evident. Nor has the ambiguity receded a great deal over the past two hundred years, since the meaning of the Reagan administration's New Federalism is far from clear to observers in the 1980s. It is the purpose of this volume, at the very least, to clarify some of the ambiguities surrounding federalism as a concept. The essays in this volume will consider the historical origins of federalism in the United States; trace its evolution from the Constitutional Convention of 1787 to the Reagan administration; and finally compare the American version of federalism with that of another federal state with a new constitution of its own, Canada. This exercise has a broader purpose, however. We will be viewing many of these developments from the unique perspective of George Mason.

To commemorate the role of George Mason in such events as the writing of the United States Constitution and the Bill of Rights, events whose bicentennials will soon be celebrated, George Mason University is sponsoring an annual lecture series. The fourth in this series, on the subject *Federalism*, was presented in the spring of 1985. These lectures, part of a projected series of ten volumes, are published annually as *The George Mason Lectures*.

I

Federalism was a system of government with which Americans had virtually no experience during their lives as British colonists. True, some may have been familiar with the operation of the Iroquois Confederation and those with good libraries and the leisure and inclination to read, such as George Mason, may have had a theoretical knowledge of a variety of governmental forms. However, the great majority of colonists had never lived under a system other than the British. As Linda Grant DePauw points out in her essay, the Americans, especially at moments of crisis, had met to create partial or complete colonial unions, along with governing systems which would have divided responsibilities—if not power—between the British government and the colonial legislatures. While the short-lived New England Confederation shrank from intruding on the sovereignty of King or Parliament, plans of union created by William Penn and Benjamin Franklin contained a colonial congress or grand council which sought to share power with the colonial administrators in London.

Two difficulties stood in the way of such schemes. Agreement was widespread, at least among European theorists, that sovereignty could not be divided—or it would cease to be sovereignty. Thus British officials would never agree to any of the colonial schemes. Furthermore, Americans were so divided that there seemed little likelihood of these virtually independent thirteen entities ever working together of their own volition. J. Hector St. John De Crèvecoeur may have felt that there was "the American, this new man," present in the colonies by 1782, but if George Gallup were living then, and conducting one of his famous polls on the subject, it is doubtful that many colonists would have agreed with Crèvecoeur's assessment that a feeling of Americanism was prevalent. Their principal loyalties, if not to the mother country, were more than likely to town, county, colony, or section. Whether it be Bacon's Rebellion in Virginia, the Paxton Boys uprising in Pennsylvania, or the Regulators in North Carolina, it was apparent that Piedmont versus Tidewater style differences within colonies often put residents of the same colony at odds with each other. These problems might revolve around: (1) religion, since dissenting religious sects often settled on the frontier; (2) absence of such government services on the frontier as military protection and court sessions; (3) lack of adequate transportation, which led to problems in marketing western goods as well as attending courts and assemblies meeting in the eastern section of most colonies; (4) payments of poll taxes, quitrents, and whiskey excise taxes—all with an inadequate amount of specie along the frontier; (5) land dealings by Tidewater speculators which made eastern lands unaffordable for many forced to move to the frontier. When one crossed colonial boundary lines, such internal problems were magnified by intercolonial rivalries such as boundary disputes, so dramatically recounted in Dixon Ryan Fox's *Yankees and Yorkers*.

Therefore, schemes of government would have to wait until the colonists were forced to work together, when the brunt of British intrusions had reached such a point that Continental Congresses were called for 1774 and 1775. The Second Congress was in session when fighting broke out at Lexington and Concord, and continued in session while its members attempted to provide a constitutional basis for their new nation. Not until 1781 did the last of the thirteen states agree to the Articles of Confederation, and it is at this point that the student of federalism must beware of growing semantic difficulties.

Those speaking of federalism at that time period were using it synonymously with confederation, confederal, league, and alliance. Linking all these terms was a common belief that in such a system of government—and the Articles of Confederation were seen as such a system—power was retained by the constituent elements making up the federation, or confederation. What previously had been thought impossible was now being attempted by dividing sovereignty between a Confederation Congress and thirteen state governments. The division was such that the states had little to fear from Congress. They had less to fear from an executive or judicial branch of that Confederation government, since these did not exist. Article II of the new document proclaimed ultimate state sovereignty very explicitly: "Each state retains its sovereignty, freedom and independence, and every Power, Jurisdiction, and right, which is not by this confederation expressly delegated to the United States, in Congress assembled." Having fought against the sovereign in London, the Americans obviously wanted to ensure that they would not create an equally oppressive monster on their own soil. In summary then, at least until the Philadelphia Convention of 1787, a federalist was one who favored a weak central government and strong state governments.

Though the central government was properly circumscribed, questions soon developed as to whether it was not in fact hamstrung. The new government brought the war to a successful conclusion, and under its auspices the peace treaty was negotiated and ratified. Other matters facing the Confederation government, however, were not so successfully resolved. Whether it be foreign relations or economic matters at home, critics of the Articles were blaming the alleged dire straits of the new nation on the weaknesses of the central government inherent in the Articles of Confederation themselves. Subject to the most criticism was the absence of any taxing power or power to regulate commerce by the central government. The Congress could only requisition the states for funds, with no satisfactory way of compelling the states to respond, while commercial regulations were left entirely with the state governments.

How poorly the nation fared in the 1780s, and whether its fate in fact could be attributed to failures in the Articles, have been subjects of considerable historical dispute. That popular expositor of virtually all subjects in the late nineteenth century, John Fiske, labeled the decade of the eighties as "the critical period of American history" in an 1888 book of the same title. In a chapter titled "Drifting Toward Anarchy," Fiske wrote about "the wretched state of things which followed the Revolution." He concluded that "we seemed to be treading the old-fashioned paths of anarchy," and it was only the Constitution that saved us from "untold dangers and horrors."[3] Charles and Mary Beard noted in 1927 that: "The chief sources of information bearing on this thesis are the assertions and lamentations of but one faction in the great dispute and they must, therefore, be approached with the same spirit of prudence as Whig editorials on Andrew Jackson or Republican essays on Woodrow Wilson."[4] Going further than the Beards in his attempt to present a revisionist interpretation of the Confederation Era, University of Wisconsin historian Merrill Jensen deliberately sought evidence from supporters of the Confederation as well as their more vocal and energetic detractors. He concludes, in *The New Nation*, that the Confederation government was indeed maligned.[5] While this controversy is only of tangential interest for this volume, it is significant for us that the nation's economic health became a pretext—whether justified or not—for altering the Confederation government, drafting an entirely new form of government, and at the same time arguing that federalism was not only being retained, but strengthened.

Nationalists, for want of a better label, had sought since the birth of the Articles to provide a stronger national government for the young nation. They created departments, such as foreign affairs, finance, and war, which gave a degree of added strength to the Confederation. They sought to join unpaid soldiers with public creditors in an attempt to threaten the states into expanding the powers of Congress, but to no avail when the soldiers were sent home on indefinite "furlough" in June 1783.[6] Most often tried and failed were attempts to amend the Articles, requiring unanimous agreement of the states, to provide Congress an import duty as a source of independent revenue. Failing in these efforts, nationalists sought another approach, this time bypassing Congress by calling separate meetings of state representatives. It is at this point that George Mason enters the story.

Mason had not been known as a nationalist, at least through the first half of the 1780s. Indeed, all of his inclinations led him in the other direction. Mason's world was bounded, as his biographer Helen Hill Miller notes, "by a triangle with points at Alexandria, Williamsburg, and Richmond."[7] If possible, he preferred to stay at one point in the triangle, his exquisite estate of Gunston Hall on the Northern Neck of the Potomac, a short way from his friend and neighbor at Mount Vernon, George Washington. Mason is reminiscent of Agatha Christie's famous sleuth, Miss Marple, who gained her great knowledge of the world and its people from her observations made at home, in St. Mary Mead. So Mason stayed at home on his plantation, personally overseeing its operations, nursing the gout which developed by his thirties and worsened throughout his life, and tending to his nine surviving children (alone, after the death of his first wife in 1773, until his remarriage in 1780).

While his education had been provided by tutors, his uncle possessed a fine library which Mason used extensively in a program of self-education that produced one of the finest minds of the revolutionary generation. His provincialism was therefore tempered by an academic knowledge of the world, so thorough in law, for instance, that his legal opinions were sought most avidly—even by lawyers. If Mason could engage in public service which did not require travel, he was receptive. Thus he served as vestryman of his Anglican parish, justice of the peace of Fairfax County, and a member of his local militia company.

After a brief service as burgess at Williamsburg in 1759–1760, he was ready to return to more local affairs, when the struggle against Britain brought him more frequent service in his colonial (later state) assembly. Here Mason distinguished himself by his drafts of the Virginia Declaration of Rights (included in the Appendix of this volume) as well as the Virginia Constitution. Whether due to a genuine illness or a convenient ailment useful to avoid unpleasant journeys, Mason not surprisingly refused to accept service in the Continental Congress. The Articles of Confederation, therefore, were not the result of his pen. They were, however, sufficiently federal and republican to meet Mason's standards. In December 1783 James Madison queried Mason on the subject of a conference to revise the Articles, finding him "sound and ripe. . . . His heterodoxy lay chiefly in being too little impressed with either the necessity or the proper means of preserving the confederacy."[8] Three years later, Madison reported to Thomas Jefferson that he was fearful of Mason's "federal ideas."[9] Perhaps Madison was justifiably fearful. Indicative of Mason's views during this period are Fairfax County's instructions to its Assembly delegates, drafted by Mason: "We desire and instruct you strenuously to oppose all encroachments of the American Congress upon the sovereignty and jurisdiction of the separate States; and every assumption of power, not expressly invested in them, by the Articles of Confederation."[10]

Events were soon to throw Mason directly in the path of constitutional reform, and lead him to take the longest trip of his life, 140 miles to Philadelphia. This route started, appropriately, at the local level over an issue about which he long had been concerned, regulations governing navigation and fishing on the Potomac River. Robert Rutland, Mason's biographer and editor of the Mason Papers, finds it conceivable that a conference was planned at Alexandria in 1785 so that Mason would have no excuse for failure to appear as a Virginia delegate.[11] Due to the often faulty communication of the time, Mason learned of his appointment as a commissioner by "mere Accident" only two or three days prior to the planned date of the meeting with Maryland's commissioners. Invited to meet at Mount Vernon, two Virginia and three Maryland commissioners found themselves agreeing so amicably that they quickly drew up a compact. Mason was thus at the first of three meetings which nationalists were to use as a method for bypassing Congress in order to strengthen the Confederation.

Madison used the opportunity to push a resolution through the Virginia House of Delegates calling for another convention, to meet in the fall of 1786 at Annapolis, to which all states were invited to send delegates to discuss commercial matters. Madison explained to Jefferson that "It was thought prudent to avoid the neighborhood of Congress, and the large Commercial towns, in order to disarm the adversaries to the object, of insinuations of influence from either of these quarters."[12] Apparently not all suspicions were stilled, for merchant Stephen Higginson suspected that the object of the Annapolis Convention was more political than commercial, for few of the Convention leaders had "been in the commercial line, nor is it probable they know or care much about commercial objects."[13] Privately, Madison revealed to Jefferson that he agreed with the goal of making "this meeting subservient to a plenipotentiary Convention for amending the Confederation."[14] At the very least, it might prepare the public mind for more radical changes in the governmental structure.

Mason missed what would have been an historic opportunity to attend each of the three gatherings in the creation of the Constitution, since he rejected his appointment to represent Virginia at Annapolis. Four of the five states which sent delegates had provided written instructions limiting their powers to improving state commercial relations—the avowed purpose of the convention. Only New Jersey had empowered her commissioners "to consider how far a uniform system in their commercial regulations and other important matters might be necessary to the common interest and permanent harmony of the several states."[15] The dozen delegates appeared to share the same opinion—that the federal power must be increased. Perhaps the opponents of this idea stayed at home rather than present themselves as delegates from their states. Significantly, the report, though presumably written by Alexander Hamilton, was issued under the signature of the New Jersey delegate, the only one empowered by his state to deal with "other important matters." It recommended that a further convention be held, whose delegates would have powers similar to those given by New Jersey, so that they could alter the Confederation in such ways "as shall appear to them necessary to render the constitution of the Federal government adequate to the exigencies of the Union."[16] Now what many people had secretly desired was openly declared. Regulating commerce was so intermeshed with all the other powers of government that a general convention was needed to remedy the Confederation.

The Annapolis resolutions were sent to the Congress where it was hoped they would be sanctioned and passed on to the state legislatures. By that time, the idea of a convention was nothing new to the members of Congress, since they had frequently flirted with the notion. At least two issues had stymied action: who legally should propose amendments to the Articles and what was the intent of those striving for such amendments. Though the Annapolis resolutions stimulated action from Congress, ironically they never heard a motion to consider the Annapolis proposals. For reasons still unclear, both New York and Massachusetts introduced resolutions almost identical to the Annapolis ones, and the Massachusetts resolution was approved on 21 February 1787. In wording now quite familiar, the motion called for a convention the following May in Philadelphia for the purpose of making such alterations in the Articles "as shall . . . render the federal Constitution adequate to the exigencies of government and the preservation of the Union."[17] In light of future events, it appears that Nathan Dane's speech to the Massachusetts House of Representatives expressed a well-founded skepticism of the Annapolis proposals:

> It does not fully appear whether they had it in contemplation to do away the present system, and to adopt another on different principles, and with different features, or to Preserve the principles and great out-lines of the present, and to make some alterations in it, to give it more strength and energy. If the latter is intended, may it not be best to consider the progress already made in amending the present system? If the former, will it not be best to ask if the public mind is prepared for it?[18]

To ensure that George Mason would attend the Philadelphia gathering, Virginia's Governor Edmund Randolph wrote him three times and Mason actually received one of the notifications. While the instructions that the various states provided their delegates varied considerably, Virginia's was certainly one of the most liberal in the discretion it gave its delegation. Initially, Mason seemed in tune with the rest of the delegation. Reporting to his son on some early caucusing by the Virginia delegation prior to the opening of the full Convention, Mason seemed receptive to the ideas being circulated:

> The most prevalent Idea, in the principal States seems to be a total Alteration of the present foederal System and substituting a great National Council, or Parliament, . . . and to make the several State Legislatures subordinate to the National, by giving the latter the Power of a Negative upon all such Laws, as they shall judge contrary to the Interest of the foederal Union. It is easy to foresee that there will be much Difficulty in organizing a Government upon this great Scale, & at the same time reserving to the State Legislatures a sufficient Portion of Power for promoting & securing the Prosperity & Happiness of their respective Citizens. Yet, with a proper Degree of Coolness, Liberality & Candour (very rare Commodities by the Bye) I doubt not but it may be effected.[19]

The quotations with which this Introduction began suggest that one of the issues which proved most divisive at the Convention involved the retention of a federal system of government. If, as became quickly apparent, the great majority of delegates preferred to ignore the existing Articles and create an entirely new structure, could that new structure be made in such a way as to keep the federal virtues of the Articles? If a strong, national government were created, as in fact nationalists had been seeking for several years, then would not such a consolidated or unitary government be the death of federalism? While George Mason was an outspoken participant at the Convention and obviously had opinions on a wide range of subjects, his opinions on the nature of federalism are of principal interest for our purposes. Indeed, Mason is an ideal choice, since he was as concerned about this as any of the other fifty-four delegates; and it was partly this concern which led him to withhold his signature on the final document, along with only two other delegates then in Philadelphia.

Mason's feelings on this subject developed slowly. On June 7, for example, while speaking in favor of the election of senators by state legislatures, he insisted that: "The State Legislatures also ought to have some means of defending themselves agst. encroachments of the Natl. Govt. . . . . And what better means can we provide than the giving them some share in, or rather to make them a constituent part of, the Natl. Establishment." He noted that the delegates were familiar with the evils of excessive state power, but what evils might arise from excessive national power "remain to be displayed."[20] A few weeks later he noted in debate "that notwithstanding his solicitude to establish a national Government, he never would agree to abolish the State Govts. or render them absolutely insignificant. They were as necessary as the Genl. Govt. and he would be equally careful to preserve them."[21] By August 31 Madison records Mason's most intemperate outburst: "He [Mason] would sooner chop off his right hand than put it to the Constitution as it now stands."[22] Never a man known for an excess of patience, Mason's quota of patience at this point in the hot Philadelphia summer must have reached its limit over the federal–national issue as well as several others which troubled him.

Most serious, and related to the subject of federalism, was the absence of a bill of rights in the new Constitution. He argued that state bills of rights were not sufficient guarantees of liberty under a governmental system which made federal laws and treaties paramount to both state laws and state bills of rights.[23] When a motion for such an addition to the draft Constitution was defeated on September 12, Mason's opposition became determined. Three days later he was casting "animadversions on the dangerous power and stucture of the Government, concluding that it would end either in monarchy, or a tyrannical aristocracy." He repeated his now familiar call for another convention to reconsider all these issues, and the following day sketched his "Objections To This Constitution Of Government," a document soon to be widely distributed—and criticized—by his political opponents.[24]

It is the nature of the opposition that lends considerable confusion to the subject of federalism. Madison reported that "Col. Mason left Philada. in an exceeding ill humour indeed."[25] His humor was certainly not helped by a carriage accident near Baltimore, which left Mason bloodied and added further complications to his already lengthy litany of ailments. But when he had time to reflect on recent events, one conclusion casts some light on the meaning of federalism. Writing the following spring, he referred to "The Federalists, as they improperly style themselves."[26] Improper it may have been, but good politics it certainly was also. Supporters of the new federal Constitution, nationalists in the years prior to the Philadelphia Convention, now wished to convince the public that their new government was not a radical break with the past but was in fact still a federal system. They therefore called themselves Federalists. While Antifederalists like George Mason did not believe this contention, they found their faction saddled with a very inappropriate name, and one not at all indicative of their true position on federalism. To people like Mason, they were the true—and indeed only—federalists. They were certainly not anti-federalism; they were anti-Constitution. Yet their opponents, the Federalists, had usurped their name, even as the Federalists had taken over the Constitutional Convention itself.

Who, after all the gatherings and seemingly hollow rhetoric of the 1780s, expected anything to come from the newest meeting at Philadelphia? Who were those most eagerly advancing their candidacy as delegates to the Convention; who had the clearest agenda to bring with them to Philadelphia? Conversely, who were those most content to remain at home, happy in the operation of a confederation government that gave their local and state governments ultimate sovereignty? The latter were, of course, people like Mason himself, though he was the exception who actually came to Philadelphia, however reluctant he was to travel. Patrick Henry, another Antifederalist, had refused to participate because he "smelt a rat." Others smelled nothing but a waste of their time on a fruitless convention, and so stayed home. Even such an ardent nationalist, and later equally ardent Federalist, as Madison was overcome by such black doubts about the outcome of the Convention that he suggested that General Washington delay his arrival at Philadelphia "until some judgment can be formed of the result of the meeting," since he did not wish Washington's glory tarnished by an "abortive undertaking."[27] Of the New York City newspapers then circulating, neither the *Packet*, *Daily Advertiser*, nor *Journa*l announced anything more about the selection of delegates to Philadelphia than: "by joint ballot of the senate and assembly, the . . . [names] were chosen delegates." A record of the votes in the Senate was not even published.[28]

Having created a revolutionary new government, and armed with their new name linking them with the past government, Federalists sought to justify their actions—and their name—as the ratification process began. Along with the new document, they presented the President of the Congress with an explanation claiming: "It is evidently impracticable in the Federal government of these states to secure all rights of independent sovereignty to each and yet provide for the interest and safety of all."[29] Further, they argued that it would have been improper to delegate such a vast amount of new powers, as was required to remedy defects in the existing government, to a Confederation with only a one-house Congress. Thus they rationalized going far beyond the existing Articles.

Perhaps their best exposition on the issue of federalism came in Nos. 39 and 40 of *The Federalist*, both written by Madison. After examining the Constitution in a variety of ways, Madison concedes that "The proposed Constitution . . . is, in strictness, neither a national nor a federal Constitution, but a composition of both." He further examines the wording of the state credentials, in most cases allowing delegates "to frame a *national government*, adequate to the *exigencies of government*, and *of the Union*; and to reduce the articles of Confederation into such form as to accomplish these purposes." He supposes that "a *national* and *adequate government* could not possibly, in the judgment of the convention, be effected by *alterations* and *provisions* in the *articles of Confederation*." If not, then "which part of the definition ought to have been embraced and which rejected? Which was the more important, which the less important part? Which the end; which the means?" Madison answered his own questions. The most important part of the instructions, to which all the rest must give way, was the forming of "a *national government*, adequate to the *exigencies of government*, and *of the Union*."[30]

Madison was suggesting, in fact, that a new form of government was being created by the Constitution. It would be called federalism forever after, to the pique of Mason and his fellow Antifederalists, as several of the essays in this volume elucidate. Mason refused to accept this redefinition of a theory of government he held dear. Fighting his final battle at the Virginia ratifying convention, he argued that "whether the constitution be good or bad, . . . it is a national government, and no longer a confederation." Congress' new taxing power would "entirely change the confederation of the states into one consolidated government. . . . The very idea of converting what was formerly a confederation, to a consolidated government, is totally subversive of every principle which has hitherto governed us. This power is calculated to annihilate totally the state governments."[31]

Though Mason would not admit that a new federalism was evolving, his objections were not without result. Except for constitutional specialists and those Virginians who luxuriate in their commonwealth's history, too few people realize that it was the emphasis of Mason and his Antifederalist cohorts on a bill of rights which convinced the Federalists to append such a document to the Constitution quickly, in order to prevent a threatened second convention. Mason's Virginia Declaration of Rights was, in fact, the model for the federal Bill of Rights. Mason failed with one proposed amendment, however, which he hoped would return the new government to true principles. He sought to adopt the wording of Article II of the former Confederation government, so "That each State in the Union shall retain its Sovereignty, Freedom and Independence, and every Power, Jurisdiction and Right, which is not by this Constitution expressly delegated to the Congress of the United States."[32] The Tenth Amendment of the Constitution is similar in tone, but with subtle differences that would never satisfy Mason.

II

The first three of the papers that follow explore the origins and development of federalism in the United States, taking both historical and political science perspectives. Linda Grant DePauw, author of "The Roots of American Federalism," is professor of American History at The George Washington University. She has written extensively on subjects relating to the Revolutionary Era, since her Beveridge Award winning first book, *The Eleventh Pillar: New York State and the Federal Constitution.* As director of the First Federal Congress Project for almost twenty years, she supervised publication of the initial volumes in the *Documentary History of the First Federal Congress, 1789–1791.*

DePauw examines America up to and including the writing and ratification of the Constitution. She examines those factors which separated the colonists, including such ever-present phenomena as abominable roads hindering even minimal travel and communication. Yet she also considers the development of ethnic pluralism and the beginnings of pride in America's melting-pot characteristics. Despite the common political heritage of the British colonists, such schemes as the New England Confederation and the Albany Plan of Union still failed.

DePauw examines the operation of the Articles of Confederation, noting particularly the spate of "unconstitutional conventions" which were called by various states throughout the decade of the eighties, in violation of the Articles themselves. She gives particular attention to the three conventions most famous for creating the Constitution: the Mount Vernon Conference, the Annapolis Convention, and the Philadelphia Convention of 1787. She points out the potential for disaster for the new nation if such an unconstitutional gathering as the one at Philadelphia were to fail. DePauw analyzes both the winning arguments of the Federalists, and also the Whig arguments used by a number of Antifederalists.

Indeed, a final irony is noted: not long after its passage, people of all political complexions joined in what became virtually a form of Constitution worship. The arguments of the losers were submerged for many generations by this frenzied veneration of a patriotic symbol. While the Federalists deserve adulation for their superb creation, one might be mindful of what John Adams thought of such symbols (at least those from which he was omitted): "The history of our Revolution will be one continued Lye from one end to the other. The essence of the whole will be *that Dr. Franklin's electrical Rod, smote the Earth and out sprung General Washington. That Franklin electrified him with his rod—and thence forward these two conducted all the Policy, Negotiations, Legislatures and War.*"[33]

Looking at many of the same issues from the perspective of a political scientist, Daniel J. Elazar provides a different approach to the issue of federalism in the second essay, "Mason Versus Madison: Developing an American Theory of Federal Democracy." As professor of Political Science and director of the Center for the Study of Federalism at Temple University, Elazar's professional career centers around this issue. He is the editor of *Publius: The Journal of Federalism*. His books include *American Federalism: A View from the States*.

Comparing Madison and Mason as philosophers of government, Elazar finds himself on the side of Madison and his views of republicanism and federalism. Yet Elazar feels there is much worth remembering from Mason's critique of the Constitution, which in several instances has turned out to be correct in its prophecies. We are reminded of the contemporary differences between confederation and federation, differences which the Federalists eventually eliminated by their successful blending of both concepts into the new federal Constitution, forever after seen as the epitome of federalism. In analyzing the species of federalism and such of its genera as federation and confederation, Elazar notes that both sides in the Constitutional debates had a misperception of the other. Just as Mason and his Antifederalist colleagues refused to concede that the new government was a successful blend of the older confederal with the newer federal ideas, so Madison and the Federalists saw the existing confederation as nothing but an old-fashioned, even feudal, league or alliance, when in fact it had evolved considerably from that antique heritage.

To any reader not familiar with the Federalist-Antifederalist debates, an explanation at this point may be valuable concerning an editorial decision to capitalize these words throughout the text. In the debates over the nature of the Confederation government prior to the meeting at Philadelphia, nationalists sought to strengthen the central government while federalists were content with the "federal" nature of the Articles. Since these groups were in a shifting, inchoate form which did not yet have any real issue around which to coalesce, they are simply names describing a common way of thinking and have not been capitalized. Once an issue was presented, ratification of the Constitution, these two groups crystallized into bodies which, though not yet deserving the title of political parties, would at least be the equivalent of the contemporary "faction." To recognize this transformation into competing political factions, it is appropriate to capitalize their names—Federalists and Antifederalists.

Another word to the reader newly entering the oft-times confusing Confederation-Constitutional Era. Elazar, as well as the other authors in this volume, has wisely chosen to circumvent the historiographical debate concerning the nature of the Confederation government. Alluded to earlier in this Introduction, its extreme positions are taken by John Fiske, portraying the Confederation as a "critical period," and Merrill Jensen attempting to present the Confederation in a more positive light. While Elazar attempts to strike a middle-ground on this issue, he does not agree with the implications of the Jensen-Beard Thesis.

Some Progressive historians have constructed a virtual conspiracy theory of the writing and ratification of the Constitution, suggesting that the federalist supporters of the Confederation government were somehow more radical in their political outlook, while the nationalists were more conservative in their views. The assumption, in barest outline, is that the federalists wanted power retained at the local and state levels so that these governments, closest to the people, could be kept most responsive to the will of the people. Thus these federalists, and their chosen form of government—the Articles of Confederation—become the more democratic of the two factions in the eighties. Conversely, the nationalists are pictured as seeking a central government strong enough to replace the lost authority of London so that their property, commercial transactions, and land speculations would continue to receive all necessary governmental protection. They are therefore depicted as promoting the less democratic, though stronger, constitutional form of government. Though an intriguing dramatization of events, Cecelia Kenyon suggests not only that there was little difference between the two groups, but that the federalists/Antifederalists may indeed have been less democratic in their approach to government than the nationalists/Federalists.[34] The intricacies of this debate are well beyond the scope of the present volume.

As chairman of the Advisory Commission on Intergovernmental Relations, Robert B. Hawkins, Jr. provides both an academic and a quite practical approach to the subject of federalism in his essay, "Federalism: The Contemporary Challenge." In California, he served as chair of the Governor's Task Force on Local Government Reform and director of the California State Office of Economic Opportunity. He has been a member of the President's Federalism Advisory Committee as well as a fellow at the Hoover Institution, the Woodrow Wilson International Center for Scholars, and the Center for the Study of Federalism and a frequent contributor to its journal, *Publius: The Journal of Federalism*. He is presently the President and Chief Executive Officer of the Institute for Contemporary Studies in San Francisco.

In his paper, Hawkins is drawing extensively from the research of the Advisory Commission on Intergovernmental Relations (ACIR). This is a bipartisan body of twenty-six members, created by Congress in 1959 to monitor the operations of the federal system. Its members, most of whom are appointed by the President, represent the executive and legislative branches of all levels of government, as well as the public. Studies undertaken by the ACIR have included assessments of taxing practices, transportation issues, structural relationships among the various governments, and indeed any issue which appears amenable to the staff, budget and methods of the Commission.

Hawkins takes the issue of federalism through the upheavals of the nineteenth century and considers the present condition of the federal–state–local relationship. Labeling the era from 1789 to 1929 as one of Dual Federalism, Hawkins takes the traditional view of this era. Dual Federalism suggests a clear separation among the levels of government, with any interaction a rare phenomenon. Certainly it was in the interest of southern pro–slavery advocates to keep the federal government from any intrusions that might endanger their "peculiar institution." In the late nineteenth century it was similarly to the advantage of business interests, promoting *laissez–faire* as the divinely ordained economic policy of the nation, to keep the spheres of governmental activity separate and thus unable to intervene in their economic affairs. Yet in his essay, Elazar labels the Jefferson Presidency as a period of Cooperative Federalism because of the financial policies of Treasury Secretary Albert Gallatin. Though neither author concentrates on the nineteenth century in this volume, it is apparent that some disagreement exists regarding the nature of nineteenth century federalism.

In his book *The American Partnership: Intergovernmental Cooperation in the Nineteenth–Century United States*, Elazar expands his thesis that Cooperative Federalism in fact began in the nineteenth century, though a dichotomy between its theory and practice has kept us from appreciating its presence. He suggests that Dual Federalism may be like late nineteenth century *laissez–faire* in that both were paid lip–service while being frequently violated in reality. Internal improvements were an obvious field for intergovernmental cooperation, and Elazar notes the use of joint–stock companies, with stock purchased by governments and individuals, to finance assorted internal improvements, as well as create banking institutions. Building and operating asylums was frequently a cooperative venture. State school financing was often augmented by funds from the United States War Department to reimburse the states for militia-related expenses. This was not simply an exchange of funds, because states were rarely likely to tax themselves for education as they were for military purposes. Thus, the Literary Fund of Virginia was maintained, as were innumerable public colleges, through the federal land grant system begun in 1862 by the Morrill Act. Whether such cooperative ventures were widely known or refined to twentieth century standards, evidence of some early Cooperative Federalism does exist. Nevertheless, for the average American of the nineteenth century—and indeed of much of the twentieth century—direct contact with the federal government would come only through the daily appearance of the postman, unless military service was involved.

Hawkins concedes that the seeds of a new era developed at least by the end of this period of Dual Federalism, since federal taxation and intergovernmental aid programs were expanding in the decades prior to 1930. By 1930, Hawkins sees a new era at hand, one he can accept as Cooperative Federalism. It began with Herbert Hoover's attempts to deal with the depression and was followed by the New Deal and its heirs, both Democratic and Republican. With Lyndon Johnson and his Great Society, Hawkins finds an era of Overloaded Federalism beginning in 1964 and continuing until the advent of the Reagan administration. Whereas federal grants and regulations began to dominate both state and local governments in the period of Cooperative Federalism, Hawkins argues that these became so intrusive as to provoke a confrontational atmosphere by the era of Overloaded Federalism. Ignoring Richard Nixon's call in 1969 for a New Federalism in which power, funds and responsibility were to be returned to the states and the people from Washington, Hawkins also gives short shrift to the only achievement of this early version of New Federalism, revenue-sharing. Despite some tentative turning from specially earmarked federal grants for particular categories of state and local programs (categorical grants) to "no-strings" awards (block grants), Hawkins concludes that this pre-Reagan administration period of Overloaded Federalism was generally one in which "federal intrusion was pervasive and deep."

Only the period since 1981, the era of New Federalism in Hawkins' nomenclature, is depicted as one in which there has been a genuine effort to reverse federal dominance. Whether this reincarnated New Federalism will fare better than the Nixon original remains to be seen. If responsibilities are returned to state and local governments without the funds to carry them out, then either government officials must find new sources of revenue or dispense with the programs. Much has been made in the eighties of a renaissance of state and local governments. Supreme Court reapportionment decisions have presumably brought a new generation into state legislatures, whose activities are now more accessible to public scrutiny as sunshine laws become more common. Though they have pioneered in new areas such as no-fault auto insurance and programs to compensate victims of crime, it is debatable whether these legislatures are quite ready for the title "laboratories of democracy" as Robert LaFollette's Wisconsin was in the early decades of this century.

In spite of a rhetorical commitment to federalism, it is also evident that some actions of the Reagan administration belie that commitment. Can federalism really be served by what is in essence a federally-mandated highway speed limit, which must be obeyed if state governments desire federal highway funds? Can the thought of federalizing state national guard units, one of the chief ornaments of state sovereignty, really be conducive to a revival of federalism? This trial balloon of the Reagan administration, aimed at overcoming some resistance to sending state militias to train in tumultuous areas of Central America—and promote the administration's foreign policy objectives—has happily been deflated. This does lead to the not very surprising suggestion that the commitment to federalism is balanced by political objectives.

Perhaps the foremost political objective of the era of New Federalism is an attempt to roll–back the social reforms of the New Deal–Fair Deal–New Frontier–Great Society years. Some political opponents of these programs have adopted the tactics of Alf Landon, Wendell Willkie and Dwight Eisenhower; namely, an acceptance of these programs and a promise to administer them in a more efficient and cost–effective manner. Others have utilized the tactics of a Robert Taft or Barry Goldwater, vowing to undo the years of reform and stage a counterrevolution of their own. By starving some of these programs under the guise of budget–cutting and deficit reduction (while refusing to accept new or increased taxes), and by returning others to the state or local levels (without returning funds as well) under the guise of federalism, the Reagan administration has found a new way of staging that long–awaited conservative counterrevolution. If programs are not killed by state and local officials starved for funds, then conservatives can hope that their grass–roots supporters will deal the finishing blow to obnoxious social programs now within their control. Thus we have come full circle from the thesis that radicals of the 1780s sought a decentralized government so they could better carry out their own—radical—agenda at the state and local levels.

The reader should be cautioned that the return to basic federal principles, which Hawkins and the ACIR recommend, must be assessed not only in light of constitutional principles and the wisdom of the Founding Fathers, but must also be considered by its potential effect on programs which the public has come to take for granted over several generations. It was, in fact, precisely because states and localities could not or would not handle certain issues that they were ultimately assumed as federal responsibilities. For example, the inter–state nature of businesses in the past century prohibited most government regulation at any level other than federal, as farm groups such as the Grange and Populists discovered when they sought to initiate state regulation of railroads in the late nineteenth century. To return programs to a more local level may be another way of killing them, or it may be a way of tailoring the programs to the needs of individual localities which best know how to deal with their local problems. Obviously Hawkins would agree with the latter position.

George Mason would more than likely agree as well. Hawkins and the ACIR are returning to some of Mason's cherished ideas. Having United States Senators chosen by state legislatures was an important part of Mason's theory of federalism. Similarly, Mason would find a pleasing enhancement of state power in Hawkins' recommendation for state-initiated Constitutional amendments.

Since the ACIR engages in studies of comparative federalism, Hawkins' paper is the first in this volume to examine in any detail federalism as practiced outside the United States. He concludes that our federal structure is less orderly than the several countries studied, and the United States has a weaker commitment to fiscal equalization than nations such as West Germany and Canada. Nevertheless, he finds that our state and local governments play a more vital role in the total governmental process than the constituent units of other federal nations. To provide a more thorough examination of one other federal system, the final paper in this volume focuses on Canada and her Constitution Act of 1982.

III

Edwin R. Black, author of the final paper, "Drunk and Disorderly: Canadian Federalism Reels into Its Second Century," is head, Department of Political Studies at Queen's University. In addition to his academic background, Black approaches his subject from the perspectives of political correspondent for various Ontario newspapers and director of the Research Office of the Official Opposition, House of Commons, Ottawa. Because Black might assume a broader knowledge of Canadian history and government from his American audience than often exists, the editor has taken several steps to clarify matters for the novice in Canadiana. A summary of events bearing on Canadian federalism prior to the Constitution of 1982 is included in this Introduction, as is an attempt to explain some of the more complex and controversial aspects of the new Constitution. Editorial annotations have been made in Professor Black's essay to clarify further any issues that might perplex an American audience, and a copy of the sixty sections of the Constitution Act of 1982 may be found in the Appendix, for the reader seeking further resources.

Canada did not approach federalism until 1841, though it would be another quarter–century before a true federal system was created. This was because Canada was not a true nation in these early years; rather, Canada was a name given by Great Britain to her collection of colonies in North America which had remained loyal to her while thirteen of her other colonies rebelled. Britain had conquered Quebec in 1760, which was then added to her domains, which already included fishing and trading colonies in Nova Scotia, Prince Edward Island, Newfoundland, and what would soon be designated New Brunswick. While some Tories, fleeing persecution from the hands of the Americans during and after the Revolutionary War, traveled to the region which became New Brunswick, it was the assumption of English administrators that the major influx of English–speaking migrants would settle in Upper Canada (Ontario) rather than the essentially Francophone Lower Canada (Quebec), "Upper" and "Lower" reflecting relationship to the St. Lawrence River.

With at least Quebec and Ontario being thought of as Canada, a Constitutional Act in 1791 established dual governments for the two provinces, reflecting and reinforcing cultural differences separating the Anglophones and Francophones. By the time that English colonial reformer Lord Durham visited Canada in 1839, abortive revolutions had been staged in both Upper and Lower Canada and conditions had deteriorated sufficiently to give rise to his most quoted remark: "I expected to find a contest between a government and a people; I found two nations warring in the bosom of a single state." Durham, who was clearly unimpressed with the Francophones and favored assimilation to proper English standards, was only calling attention to a quite obvious factor: the English had never succeeded, and rarely even tried, to assimilate the French

Canadian population. Not having been done immediately after the Conquest, it was unlikely it could be accomplished in 1839 or thereafter.

A "single state" did not even exist, except in the most theoretical sense. Therefore, the Act of Union of 1840 followed at least one of Durham's recommendations by creating the United Province of Canada, to be composed of Canada West (Ontario) and Canada East (Quebec), now joined under a single government, with the same legislature and same governor. Again, success eluded the colonial planners, for the duality of the two provinces was maintained within this purportedly single system by utilizing a method of double majorities and dual (English–French) ministries. This system might have gladdened the heart of Southern theorist of the concurrent majority, John C. Calhoun; but in practice it led to increasing instability, with ministries rising and collapsing rapidly.

As if the structural and ethnic difficulties were not sufficient, the Canadian central government faced other dilemmas. Reminiscent of the United States under the Articles of Confederation, Canada was having difficulty financing and constructing needed transportation improvements, needed at least in the opinion of those seeking faster economic development of their region. Not only was the United States outstripping Canada economically, but its interest in its "manifest destiny" was frightening to those Canadians who feared becoming another state of the United States. This fear was particularly evident after the American Civil War, when large armies might reunite and seek to retaliate for any aid that Canadians had provided to the Confederacy. All this came at a time when Britain was clearly losing interest in her North American colonies. Colonial reformers were questioning the advantages of colonies to the mother country, and such questioning had already resulted by 1849 in eliminating the famous Navigation Acts, which in a previous generation had helped to precipitate the American Revolution.

With all this in mind, politicians from almost all major parties in Canada called a truce, and created a "Great Coalition" to draft a constitution for Canada which would, they hoped, provide a lasting confederation. From this came the British North America (BNA) Act, approved by the British Parliament in 1867 as the basis for the Canadian confederation. Joined into the new Dominion—a term possibly used to avoid frightening the Americans, who so detested kingdoms or anything smacking of monarchical government—were Ontario, Quebec, New Brunswick, and Nova Scotia. By 1869 Britain had bought out the private holdings of the Hudson's Bay Company and added its vast western domain to the Dominion. Other provinces were added in subsequent years, until Newfoundland, the last holdout, joined in 1949.

The BNA Act has often been described as a businessmen's merger, with subsidies and assorted inducements doled out to entice provinces to join the union. Certainly there had been no groundswell of public support for a Dominion of Canada, nor had its "constitution" ever been ratified by any group of voters. Its organic law was a statute of the British Parliament, and any amendments had to be, likewise, British Parliamentary statutes.

Most interesting for our comparative purposes, the "fathers of confederation" sought to use the American system as a model of what *not* to do. With the American Civil War fresh in their minds, the draftsmen of the BNA Act saw the evils of a federal system that had allowed such excessive states' rights that the union itself had come close to dissolution. The Dominion, therefore, was to have its federal government so strong as to avoid these American evils. Section 91 of the BNA Act provided the clearest example of central power by allowing the federal Parliament "to make Laws for the Peace, Order, and good Government of Canada" in all fields not assigned exclusively to the provincial legislatures. Furthermore, the federal Parliament was given authority to disallow provincial legislation, which it did frequently in the first decades after confederation.

What was omitted from the BNA Act is equally significant: a bill of rights. At least, however, Canada had something close to a constitution. Following the British custom of considering its constitution as that collection of key legislative and judicial acts, along with such essential documents as the Magna Carta and the Petition of Rights, Canadians could point to the BNA Act as the centerpiece of their laws, precedents and customs which collectively became the Canadian Constitution. As one student of Canadian federalism has noted: "The Canadian Constitution [the BNA Act] at the time of its creation presented to the world of political science a novel combination of constitutional principles—a monarchical federation based upon legislative supremacy under a single external sovereign."[35] A system not drastically unlike the American federal one was, in Canada, being melded to a parliamentary government which was still, in several important ways, a colonial dependency.

One of those ways involved the Judicial Committee of the Privy Council in London serving as the final court of appeal for all Canadian judicial disputes, a practice not abandoned until 1949. A second way, eliminated at an earlier date, involved control over Canadian foreign affairs. To maintain the unity of the Empire, British statesmen assumed that one absolute essential was a unified foreign policy. This was seen as Britain's last mark of sovereignty over the dominions, and one which Englishmen were loath to renounce. Not until 1927 did Canada send her first minister, Vincent Massey, to the United States, paving the way for a fuller exchange of ministers and effectively breaking one of the last British infringements on Canadian sovereignty.[36] This status was ratified by the Statute of Westminster in 1931.

The parliamentary aspects of the Canadian government are similar to most other practitioners of this system. A House of Commons consists of members of Parliament directly elected from districts (ridings) throughout the nation. The party holding a majority of M.P.s in Commons forms a government with its party leader becoming the Prime Minister. Senators in the upper house were supposed to represent provincial or regional interests; but because their appointment was made by the Prime Minister acting through the royal representative in Canada, the Governor General, local interests have not had a strong and independent voice in the Senate. Such interests are, of course, directly represented in the ten provincial legislatures which, with their provincial premiers and lieutenant governors representing the Crown, are duplicates of the Ottawa government except for the unicameral composition of their legislatures.

This system was viewed most often as a "compact of provinces." Certainly ironic in light of the centralizing tendencies of the fathers of confederation, this compact theory acquired more than theoretical support by the end of the nineteenth century. The federal government began its tenure under the BNA Act with its strongly nationalistic first Prime Minister, Sir John A. Macdonald. But a provincial reaction soon developed to Macdonald's assertion of central supremacy. Led by Ontario, and soon joined by Quebec and most of the other provinces—all acting for quite different reasons—this "provincial rights" movement ultimately brought the Canadian system much closer to the originally despised American brand of federalism.

Richard Leach points out that "The American Constitution is founded on popular sovereignty, the BNA Act on provincial power." He suggests that "The Federalists, who carried the day at the Constitutional Convention of 1787, rooted the American Constitution in the consent of the people, a concept whose challenge to the states was immediately obvious to the Antifederalists. The Convention, Patrick Henry noted, spoke 'the language of, *We, the people*, instead of, *We, the states*.'"[37] The Canadian approach was closer to the Antifederalist position. Even the M.P. who introduced the BNA Act to the British House of Commons told the House that federation had "in this case . . . been a matter of most delicate mutual treaty and compact between the provinces."[38]

The courts soon gave their stamp of approval to this compact theory by accepting a shift in the federal–provincial balance. The Judicial Committee of the Privy Council, initially sympathetic to claims of central authority, changed later in the century. Finding less import in the aforementioned Section 91 of the BNA Act, the Privy Council now found Section 92 more significant; namely, that clause placing "Property and Civil Rights in the Provinces" under exclusive provincial jurisdiction.[39] The purpose of the BNA Act, the Privy Council said, was "neither to weld the provinces into one, nor to subordinate provincial governments to a central authority."

One result of this metamorphosis in the federal relationship, as Black indicates in his essay, is that Americans sought decentralization and got a centralized government, while Canadians, seeking centralization, got decentralization. In the full flush of provincial ascendancy, the custom developed of provinces sharing in the amending process of the BNA Act; indeed, their share became one of unanimous consent to any constitutional change. Provincial power also necessitated more formal mechanisms of intergovernmental consultation, such as periodic meetings of first ministers (the Prime Minister and provincial premiers) at the highest levels, down to exchanges of minor bureaucrats at the lower levels. This was even codified by creating a Federal–Provincial Relations Office within the Office of the Prime Minister.

Some of their former powers were regained by the federal government and its bureaucracy, as two world wars and a depression created emergency conditions grasped by Ottawa as an opportunity to assert authority. The Balfour Declaration (1926) and the Statute of Westminster (1931) had clarified Canada's role within the Commonwealth, and Canada was freely exchanging diplomats with the nations of the world in the years following 1927. Its people achieved separate Canadian citizenship (1947), began appointing Canadian-born Governors General (1952), and were flying their own Maple Leaf flag (1965). Canada had not, however, achieved federal–provincial agreement on one thing: patriation of its constitution. To bring the BNA Act home to Canada, to make it a Canadian act and remove it from the British Parliament, was a frequently sought goal and as frequently frustrated.

This issue attained a much higher profile in the 1960s. Despite a period described as Cooperative Federalism under the Liberal government of Lester Pearson, Quebec during its "Quiet Revolution" was still vying with the federal government. Such a traditional mark of cultural sovereignty as language rights was a perennial issue. Now Quebec was tangling with Ottawa over a field in which her previous governments had rarely shown any interest, social services. Quebec was belatedly entering the twentieth century world of the welfare state, and as usual attempting to go it alone. Even more dangerous for the survival of the federal union itself was the creation by former newsman and ex-Liberal René Lévesque of the Parti Québécois in 1968. Though French-Canadian nationalists previously had sought some form of provincial autonomy to allow for their separate cultural development, the electoral victory of Lévesque and his PQ party in 1976 marked the high-point of actual separatism in Quebec in the century since confederation.

As Premier of Quebec, Lévesque's plans for restructuring the federation called for Quebec to have ties only of "sovereignty-association" with the rest of Canada. The plan, put to a referendum in Quebec on 20 May 1980, called for Quebec to exercise "the exclusive power to make its laws, levy its taxes and establish relations abroad—in other words, sovereignty—and at the same time, to maintain with Canada an economic association including a common currency." Though almost sixty percent of the voters rejected a mandate for Lévesque's government to discuss this scheme, Prime Minister Pierre Trudeau had pledged during the campaign to renegotiate the terms of the federal union. His determination, more than any other single factor, brought the Constitution Act of 1982 to fruition.

Quebec was not the federal government's only problem, however. One could speak of federalism as a problem of concern only to Quebec for much of the late nineteenth and twentieth centuries. Now other provinces asserted themselves on the issue of federalism at the same time federal authorities were bedeviled by the PQ. The drastic rise in the price of oil and natural gas brought a bonanza to Alberta, for example, which would soon be quarreling with the federal government over distribution of the lucrative proceeds.

Exacerbating this problem is another alluded to by Black. Political parties in Canada had become increasingly regional rather than national. Since the days of Sir Wilfrid Laurier and of William Lyon Mackenzie King, the Liberals have been adept at alternating Anglophone with Francophone leaders, thus establishing a strong base of support in Quebec with additions from English-speaking Canada as well. In this century, then, the Prime Minister's office would most likely be held by a Liberal. By the era of Pierre Trudeau, the Liberal party was still strong in Quebec but got few Anglophone votes west of Ontario. Therefore provincial leaders, often members of an opposition party, had another bone of contention with the federal Prime Minister. Richard Hofstadter has indicated the importance of national political parties for the survival of the American union. Prior to the Civil War, American political parties became sectional rather than national; a bond of national unity was thus lost. Such a drastic fate may not await Canada in her era of sectional political parties, but the outlook is far from optimistic.

Constitutional reform was achieved within two years of the "sovereignty-association" referendum. No easier than it had ever been, this time the difference was a determined Prime Minister willing to ignore provincial objections and submit his constitution to a national referendum if necessary. Trudeau's chief goals were to patriate the constitution—bring it home to Canada and thus allow any future amendments to be a totally Canadian matter—and to "entrench" a bill of rights in the document. John Diefenbaker had managed to include a bill of rights in a 1960 Canadian Parliamentary statute, but this applied only to areas within federal jurisdiction and could easily be superseded by any future act of Parliament. To entrench a bill of rights in the constitutional document itself, making it inviolate except via the constitutional amending process, became for most Canadians the most novel feature of the new Constitution Act of 1982.

Trading Trudeau's chief priorities with provincial desires to reassess the distribution of constitutional power within the federal system, a compromise document was drafted to which nine provincial governments acceded. The Supreme Court of Canada had already reached the unusual decision that legally, unanimous provincial consent was not needed, though by convention a "substantial measure of provincial consent" was required. The definition of "substantial consent" the court prudently left to the politicians.

In April 1982 the Queen arrived in Canada to declare the Constitution Act in force. Previous constitutional legislation, such as the British North America Act, was still in effect unless otherwise indicated in the 1982 Act. Only Quebec's government refused to adhere to the new Constitution, with Lévesque asserting "we're working like mad at whatever can be done to counter the bloody thing."[40]

Whether provincial desires were met by the new Act is debatable. Federal equalization payments to the provinces, a practice followed since the beginning of confederation to redistribute funds from wealthy to less wealthy provinces, had been entrenched in the new Constitution. Provincial authority over natural resources and their sale was now confirmed. Changes which many reformers had hoped for, however, were not included. Allowing provincial parliaments to choose Senators (a reform strangely reminiscent of the ACIR's recommendation for a return to state selection of United States Senators) was omitted. No changes were introduced to allow for proportional representation of members of the House of Commons nor for a new method of selecting Supreme Court justices. Structurally, the system created by the BNA Act was still in place; the tradition of a compact among provinces had been maintained in its essential features. Most observers would agree with Richard Leach that, "In short, the new constitution does not get at the heart of the matter, the existing division of power between the national government and those of the provinces."[41]

In his essay describing Canadian federalism as it "reels into its second century," Black is most concerned not about what was left undone in the Constitution Act, but about what innovations were introduced into a system operating successfully for over a century.

Since the chief innovation was the Charter of Rights and Freedoms (taking up the first thirty–four of the sixty sections in the Constitution Act), Black focuses on issues raised by that Charter. For the non–Canadian reader, two of the most novel and unfamiliar aspects of this Charter bear further explanation. Section 1 guarantees those rights and freedoms specified in the Charter, "subject only to such reasonable limits prescribed by law as can be demonstrably justified in a free and democratic society." Whatever is meant by this "demonstrably justified" clause, its ambiguity will surely set the stage for innumerable legal battles.

More specific, and more controversial, is Section 33, the "notwithstanding clause." It allows the federal parliament or a provincial legislature to violate certain sections of the Charter of Rights and Freedoms for periods up to five years duration, as long as their legislation notes that it is being passed notwithstanding its violation of one or more clauses of the Charter. While some precedent for this type of clause can be found in several provincial bills of rights, it appears alien to United States constitutional practice. Article I, section 9, of the United States Constitution provides a slight parallel by the suspension of habeas corpus in cases of rebellion or invasion. Though a power apparently granted to Congress, Abraham Lincoln certainly made use of it during the Civil War. The Canadian "notwithstanding clause" is, however, more sweeping than this example from the United States Constitution, and may be applied in peacetime as well as wartime.

The reader is now urged to explore all these subjects further through the *George Mason Lectures* on *Federalism*.

IV

Sponsored by the Center for the Study of Constitutional Rights, the lecture series on which this volume was based was made possible by a grant from the Graduate School, George Mason University. Among those members of the University community who have been most helpful to the Project are: George W. Johnson, President; Averett S. Tombes, former Dean, the Graduate School; Ruth Kerns, Fenwick Library; Robert T. Hawkes, Jr., Dean, Division of Continuing Education; and Wayne Anderson, Department of Public Affairs. Richard B. O'Keeffe, formerly of Fenwick Library, prepared the index. We are also especially grateful to A. E. Dick Howard, University of Virginia School of Law, for his very helpful work as Chief Consultant since the project's commencement. Finally, my appreciation to two long–time colleagues and friends, Josephine Pacheco and T. Daniel Shumate, Director and Associate Director respectively of the Center, for entrusting me with their project which they have nurtured so carefully for so many years.

Martin B. Cohen

George Mason University

Notes

1. Recorded by Madison during debates of June 16, in Max Farrand, ed., *The Records of the Federal Convention of 1787.* revised ed. in 4 vols. (New Haven: Yale University Press, 1966), 1:255.

2. Ibid., 1:178; recorded by Madison during debates of June 9.

3. John Fiske, *The Critical Period of American History, 1783–1789* (Boston: Houghton, Mifflin & Co., 1899), 162, 153.

4. Charles A. Beard and Mary R. Beard, *The Rise of American Civilization* (New York: The Macmillan Co., 1936), 302. See also the classic study: Charles A. Beard, *An Economic Interpretation of the Constitution of the United States* (New York: The Macmillan Co., 1913).

5. Merrill Jensen, *The New Nation: A History of the United States During the Confederation, 1781–1789* (New York: Alfred A. Knopf, Inc., 1950).

6. Ibid., 54–58.

7. Helen Hill Miller, *George Mason: Gentleman Revolutionary* (Chapel Hill: The University of North Carolina Press, 1975), ix.

8. Robert A. Rutland, ed., *The Papers of George Mason, 1725–1792*, 3 vols. (Chapel Hill: The University of North Carolina Press, 1970), 1:cxx.

9. Ibid.

10. Ibid., 2:779–782.

11. Ibid., 3:885.

12. *Writings of James Madison*, ed. Gaillard Hunt (New York: G. P. Putnam's Sons, 1901), 227.

13. Irving Brant, *James Madison—The Nationalist*, 1780–1787 (New York: Bobbs-Merrill Co., 1948), 384.

14. *Writings of James Madison*, 262–263; 233.

15. Jonathan Elliot, ed., *Debates in the Several State Conventions on the Adoption of the Federal Constitution* (Philadelphia: J. B. Lippincott & Co., 1861), 1:117.

16. Ibid.

17. Ibid., 120.

18. Edmund C. Burnett, ed., *Letters of Members of the Continental Congress* (Washington: Carnegie Institution of Washington, 1936), 8:504.

19. Rutland, *Papers of George Mason*, 3:880.

20. Ibid., 3:902.

21. Ibid., 3:907–908.

22. Ibid., 3:973.

23. Ibid., 3:981.

24. Ibid., 3:990–993.

25. Ibid., 3:1007.

26. Ibid., 3:1040.

27. Charles Warren, *Making of the Constitution* (Boston: Little, Brown & Co., 1928), 66–67.

28. Clarence E. Miner, *Ratification of the Federal Constitution by the State of New York* (New York: Columbia University Press, 1921), 53; also see Stanley Elkins and Eric McKitrick, "The Founding Fathers: Young Men of the Revolution," *The Political Science Quarterly* 76 (June 1961): 181–216.

29. William Staples, *Rhode Island in the Continental Congress* (Providence: Providence Press Co., 1870), 583.

30. Alexander Hamilton, John Jay, and James Madison, *The Federalist* (New York: The Modern Library, n.d.), 250,252.

31. Rutland, *Papers of George Mason*, 3:1050.

32. Ibid., 3:1055; for a variety of opinions, see also Robert A. Rutland, *The Birth of the Bill of Rights, 1776–1791* (Chapel Hill: The University of North Carolina Press, 1955); Steven R. Boyd, *The Politics of Opposition: Antifederalists and the Acceptance of the Constitution* (Millwood, New York: KTO Press, 1979); Lance Banning, "Republican Ideology and the Triumph of the Constitu-

tion, 1789–1793," *William and Mary Quarterly*, 3d. ser., 31 (1974):167–188.

33. Cited in Gerald Stourzh, *Benjamin Franklin and American Foreign Policy* (Chicago: The University of Chicago Press, 1954), 5.

34. See Cecilia Kenyon, "Men of Little Faith: The AntiFederalists on the Nature of Representative Government," *William and Mary Quarterly*, 3d. ser., 12 (1955):3–43. For an excellent summation of the historiographic debate on these issues, see Elkins and McKitrick, cited in no. 28 above.

35. Canadian political scientist Frank R. Scott is the source of the quote, cited in Filippo Sabetti, "The Historical Context of Constitutional Change in Canada," in *Reshaping Confederation: The 1982 Reform of the Canadian Constitution*, ed. Paul Davenport and Richard H. Leach (Durham, No. Car.: Duke University Press, 1984), 14.

36. For further details of events surrounding the first Canadian–U.S. exchange of ministers and an assessment of its significance, see Martin B. Cohen, "The First Légation: Canadian Diplomacy and the Opening of Relations with the United States," (Ph.D. diss., The George Washington University, 1975).

37. Richard H. Leach, "Implications for Federalism of the Reformed Constitution of Canada," in *Reshaping Confederation*, ed. Davenport and Leach, 150.

38. Ibid.

39. Ibid., 151.

40. Ibid., 154–155.

41. Ibid., 159.

1

The Roots of American Federalism

LINDA GRANT DE PAUW
Professor of History
The George Washington University

FEDERATION WAS THE LAST THING CONTEMPORARIES would have expected of the British colonies in North America. Indeed, so great was the diversity of cultures in America, so frequent the disputes between colonists, so prevalent was the taste for combat, both legal and military, that it was commonly believed only the restraints imposed by common membership in the British Empire prevented violent hostilities. An English traveler who toured the colonies in 1759–1760 wrote, "Were they left to themselves, there would soon be civil war from one end of the continent to the other." Five years later another observer wrote, "Were these colonies left to themselves tomorrow, America would be a mere shambles of blood and confusion."[1]

At the time the first British colonies were planted in North America early in the seventeenth century, there was a great deal of similarity between the settlers who went to make their homes there. The first settlers of Virginia and the first settlers of New England had much in common: they were almost exclusively English, most of them from the Western districts of England, most of them lower middle class, and most of them—whether they called themselves Anglicans or Puritans—were Protestants who shared common assumptions about what was right and wrong, about the nature of the relationship between God and humanity, and about the superiority of English customs and forms of government.

But between the time of these first plantings and the Declaration of Independence, almost one hundred seventy years had passed. That is as long a period of time as has passed since the end of the War of 1812. A lot of things have changed in America since the War of 1812 and a lot of things had happened in the British colonies between the settlement of Jamestown and the establishment of the United States. The acquisition by Great Britain of North American colonies settled by other European nations and the immigration of many thousands of Europeans and Africans produced a society in British North America that was remarkable for its diversity.

By the middle of the eighteenth century, all of the North American colonies from Maine to Georgia owed allegiance to the British crown. A political map would show the entire eastern seaboard in a single color, but simply looking at such a map obscures the difficulty poor communication within that area made for those who attempted to govern. Divisions in British North America were partly caused by and certainly accentuated by geography.

In the eighteenth century no message could travel faster than a ship or a rider on horseback could carry it. And while ships had smooth sea lanes to travel—at least when there was favorable weather—travel by land was extremely slow and difficult. Most rivers had neither bridges nor ferries, and in many parts of America there were no roads at all. New England towns, for instance, had roads that enabled the settlers to go from their houses in town to their farms outside of town, but there was no attempt to build roads joining towns together. An attempt to travel from New Hampshire to Rhode Island meant, for the most part, plodding through untracked wilderness.

Even where there were roads, they were often impossible to travel on. Most of them were simply dirt roads. In the spring, when the snow melted, they became muddy trenches. The potholes were sometimes six feet deep. George Mason suffered head and neck injuries in a road accident when his coach overturned on a bad stretch of road as he was returning home from the Constitutional Convention.[2]

From a political point of view, the difficulty in travel and communication meant it was almost as difficult to convene such meetings as the Constitutional Convention as it had been for Marco Polo to make a trip to China four hundred years earlier. In fact it is possible today to get from America to China—or even to get from America to the moon—much more quickly than one could go from Virginia to New York two hundred years ago. And news, of course, travelled just as slowly.

The easy way to travel was by boat, despite the almost inevitable seasickness and dangers of shipwreck and drowning (and of capture by the enemy during wartime). It was for that reason that contact with England was easier for people in most parts of America than contact with other regions on their own continent. It was understandable, for this reason alone, for the British to assume that the American colonists could never unite.

But there were more than transportation problems standing in the way of American union. The fact was that Americans simply did not like each other very much. If one should take an imaginary trip from Maine to Georgia in the middle of the eighteenth century, one would hear a lot of the inhabitants of one locality badmouthing their neighbors. Maine, originally settled by English fishermen looking for a place to dry their catch so they could take it home to sell, was politically joined to Massachusetts—as it would be until 1820. But it had a spirit quite distinct from that of the rest of New England. The "Downeasters," as they called themselves, had little liking for the more pious New England Puritans. Puritans filled the rest of New England, but their quarrelsomeness was notorious; in tiny Rhode Island there were four major sects all battling with each other over economic and political as well as religious issues. All of New England had a bad reputation elsewhere in the colonies; a Dutch woman in New York probably spoke for most Americans outside the region when she described New Englanders as "conceited, Litigious, and selfish beyond measure, very vulgar, insolent and truly disagreeable people."[3]

The dislike, however, was mutual. The imaginary traveler crossing the Hudson River into New York would find the area still dominated by the Dutch who had established the colony in the seventeenth century. And the English detested the Dutch. They thought them materialistic and stingy. The term "Dutch treat" was a snide reference to the type of entertainment one could expect if invited to a party by the Dutch: the guest would have to pay for it. Some Englishmen became truly passionate in their dislike of these people. One wrote, "rather than marry a woman with Dutch blood in her veins whether for love or money or both united, I would ravish my grandmother, live a beggar, and die of famine in a ditch."[4]

Outsiders disliked the people of New York City as much as they disliked the upstate Dutch. John Adams of Massachusetts, who visited New York on his way to the Continental Congress, wrote: "with all the opulence and splendor of this city, there is very little good breeding to be found. I have not seen one real gentleman, one well bred man, since I came to town. At their entertainments, there is no conversation that is agreeable. There is no modesty, no attention to one another. They talk very loud, very fast, and altogether. If they ask you a question, before you can utter three words of your answer, they will break out upon you again and talk away."[5]

A traveler leaving New York and entering New Jersey would probably have no other purpose than to get through the colony as quickly as possible in order to reach Philadelphia. The people of New Jersey, who had been fighting about land titles since the Duke of York had come into possession of the territory, often complained that they felt like "a barrel tapped at both ends." All the wealth in the state seemed to flow either to the city of New York or the city of Philadelphia.

By the middle of the eighteenth century the peaceable kingdom that the Quaker William Penn had hoped to establish in Pennsylvania was far from peaceable and experienced more violent political quarrels than any other colony. Pacifist Quakers dominated Philadelphia and the seaboard; hot-blooded Indian-hating Scots-Irish settlers dominated the back country frontier. In between lived a mixture of European immigrants—Pennsylvania "Dutch"— who often isolated themselves in communities that spoke no English and had as little as possible to do with their neighbors.

South of the Mason-Dixon line defining the border between Penn's domains and the Calverts' Maryland lay the societies of the southern colonies. The South had no distinct sectional identity until the nineteenth century and was, rather, the most diverse part of the continent. In North Carolina, there was a full scale war going on in 1771 as the colonial government tried to crush a group of rebellious back country men known as the Regulators. A poor colony with an economy based on naval stores—tar, pitch, and turpentine—North Carolina had few slaves and was sometimes referred to as "a valley of humility between two mountains of conceit." The "mountain" to the north was the tobacco colony of Virginia, where the old aristocracy of "First Families" was entering hard times as the soil became depleted; and the "mountain" to the south was the booming colony of South Carolina, growing rich from rice and indigo cultivated with slave labor. Still farther south was sparsely populated Georgia, virtually a garrison state warding off threats from a large Indian population and the Spanish in Florida and Louisiana.

Outsiders, therefore, had good reasons to be skeptical of either the desire or the ability of Americans to unite for any purpose. They were, nonetheless, as we know, quite wrong. Despite what appeared to be clear evidence to contemporaries that there was no foundation for American nationhood, the Americans did, indeed, form a nation. The ethnic and cultural diversity in British North America was, in fact, less significant than it appeared, and on the level of ideas—particularly of ideas about government, law, and politics—the Americans had achieved a sense of nationality even before 1776.

Ethnic pluralism early became an element in the Americans' perception of themselves as a united people. After eight generations of living in close proximity with white settlers of other Northern European nations, Americans had begun to take pride in being the most cosmopolitan people on earth. In the twentieth century it no longer seems a triumph over racism for a society of Englishmen to manage an accommodation with Irishmen and Dutch while waging genocidal wars against Indians and holding both Indians and blacks as slaves. But for the eighteenth century, when tolerance rarely extended beyond the narrowest cultural groups, Americans might well boast of a society in which one might find "a family whose grandfather was an Englishman, whose wife was Dutch, whose son married a French woman, and whose present four sons have now wives of different nations." Hector St. John de Crèvecoeur, a French-born New York farmer, described this case, adding, "*He* is an American. . .Here individuals of all nations are melted into a new race of men."[6] Thus, while cultural conflict flourished in America on the eve of the Revolution, there was, nonetheless, a general conviction that intolerance of others was somehow un-American.

A pride in the "melting pot" was one element in early American nationalism: a common political heritage was another. The tie to England served a more positive function than merely holding civil warfare in check. English political institutions were accepted as part of the American experience and were reflected both in political institutions in all parts of British North America and in the ideas on law and government which all Americans viewed as self-evident by 1776.

Each of the thirteen colonies that joined to form the United States had approximately the same form of government during their rule by the British. A governor with viceregal powers, usually appointed by the English king (but in a few cases by proprietary families that retained rights from the time of original settlements) acted as executive head. In the eighteenth century each of these governors had engaged in a struggle over the public purse with a popularly elected colonial legislature, an institution existing in every one of the British colonies and in no other colony in the world. In so many parodies of the seventeenth century quarrels between the Stuart kings of England and the English Parliament, the colonial assemblies had established their right to initiate legislation and control public finances. Below the provincial level the colonies established various patterns of local government, but in all of these the principle of the consent of the governed was assumed. The principle of consent was, in fact, implemented more broadly in British North America than it was anywhere else in the world in the eighteenth century. Although no more than fifteen percent of the population of the colonies was actually qualified to vote, no other part of the world allowed as many as five percent to exercise an effective franchise.[7]

As the revolutionary crisis developed in the years following the Seven Years' War, Americans from all parts of the Continent appealed to the political history of seventeenth century England and to the ideas circulated by the Parliamentary party during the struggle with the Stuart kings, in order to defend their own self-governing practices against what they believed to be unconstitutional British innovations. The cohesion of the revolutionary movement was first built on the level of political and constitutional theory. When discussing the question of taxation without representation, New England shopkeepers and Virginia plantation owners found they shared a large body of common political principles.

Finally, in the fall of 1774, the crisis following the Boston Tea Party and the imposition of sanctions on Boston as punishment, supplied the impetus for the meeting of the First Continental Congress. Perhaps the most important achievement of the Congress was to bring fifty-six gentlemen from different sections of America to Philadelphia where they could talk together, dine together, and discover that their sectional prejudices were far less important than they had supposed.

The business of the First Continental Congress, as they saw it, was to heal the breach with England. They were not successful, and before the Second Continental Congress convened in May 1775, the "shot heard round the world" had been fired in Lexington and the War for American Independence had begun.

The Continental Congress did not entertain a motion to declare independence from Great Britain for more than a year after the Revolutionary War began, but the existence of the Congress itself presumed the existence of a colonial union. And Benjamin Franklin proposed the adoption of Articles of Confederation and Perpetual Union in 1775. Such a document was not drafted at that time only because members of Congress considered it premature to adopt a constitution before they had decided whether or not they intended to become an independent nation. But a committee was appointed to draft the Articles on the very same day a committee was appointed to draft a Declaration of Independence.

This first written constitution for the United States took only a month to draft, although it was not formally ratified by all the states until 1781. Nevertheless, Americans behaved as though it were in effect from the time it was introduced, and the "confederation and perpetual union" thus formed held together well enough to carry the nation through eight years of war and several years of peace.

The idea of forming a confederation of colonies was not new. The need for unity had always been particularly apparent in wartime—and war with Indian nations and their French or Spanish allies had been almost continuous from the time British settlements appeared on the Continent. During these colonial wars, membership in the British Empire was of little practical value, although it often was the decisive factor in setting off renewed conflicts after an interval of peace. The burden of defense during King William's War, Queen Anne's War, the Yamasee War, and countless unnamed and undeclared wars was placed on individual frontier families. Neither British troops nor regularly organized colonial troops did much of the fighting, and although there were hundreds of thousands of British settlers involved in these wars, their military effectiveness was hampered by lack of central control. The solution was cooperation—and confederation.

In 1643 the colonies of Massachusetts, Plymouth, Connecticut and New Haven ratified articles of confederation by which they agreed to form The United Colonies of New England. Commissioners from these four colonies continued to meet until 1684. And there were many other proposals for intercolonial union.

The last such plan proposed before the Revolution was known as the Albany Plan of Union. The Albany Plan was drawn up by Benjamin Franklin during a period of peace on the assumption that there would be another war very soon. His proposal was discussed at a meeting at Albany, New York in 1754, but the colonies felt no urgency. Virginia and New Jersey did not even send delegates to attend the meeting. Two years later Virginia was left to fight her part of the Seven Years' War without much help from her neighbors in either the Carolinas or Maryland. Whig political theory, the "self-evident truths" of the eighteenth century, suggested that free people should never delegate more than the minimum power necessary to governors of any sort. Consequently, those colonial assemblies that voted on the Albany Plan of Union rejected it.

None of the early plans for union assumed independence for the colonies. They were primarily directed to solving common problems of frontier defense and occasionally problems of commerce. The men who had supported such proposals over the decades, however, had repeatedly recommended the same basic structure: a central executive who would govern in conjunction with a legislative body made up of delegates appointed by the individual colonial legislatures. No wonder, then, that when some central political organization became essential because the colonies had made the decision to withdraw from the British empire, this traditional structure was adopted.

The government of the Articles of Confederation was federal in the strict sense of the word. Thirteen states of unequal wealth and population were represented equally in a Congress composed of members elected by and responsible to state legislatures. The restrictions placed on the states and the powers granted to the central government were clearly defined, and it was explicitly stated that "Each state retains its sovereignty, freedom, and independence, and every power, jurisdiction, and right which is not by this confederation expressly delegated to the United States in Congress assembled." Individual states were forbidden to make foreign alliances without Congressional consent, to levy tariffs not countenanced by Congressional treaties, or to maintain any military or naval force in peacetime without consent of Congress. Congress was empowered to declare war, make peace, send and receive ambassadors, negotiate treaties, and to appoint most military and naval officers. On the domestic side, Congress regulated the currency, established post offices, and held the final appeal in interstate boundary disputes.

Under the Articles of Confederation, the United States won its independence from Great Britain and survived the first difficult years as a new nation. Those first years would have been difficult under any constitution. Having divorced herself from the British Empire, the most powerful international power of its day, the United States found herself deprived of the economic and political advantages membership in that Empire had conferred. The usual wartime inflation was followed by the usual post–war depression, which those whose economic interests extended beyond the boundaries of a subsistence farm suffered unusually keenly because the familiar cycle was this time accompanied by disruption of traditional trade relations, disorganized credit, and political uncertainty.

The Articles of Confederation were not responsible for the difficulties the United States experienced in the years immediately following independence. The difficulties stemmed directly from the realities of international power; the United States was a tenth–rate nation and was treated accordingly. The minority of Americans whose financial interests kept them interested in international affairs even in peacetime, however, blamed their constitution. Dissatisfaction with foreign affairs was probably the strongest impulse for Constitutional reform in the 1780's. Congress lacked the power to levy direct taxes and, therefore, it was said, the public credit suffered. Congress did not have exclusive control of commerce, it could not levy duties on imports and exports, therefore it could not offer concessions or threaten reprisals in order to gain commercial advantages abroad. Congress had neither the money nor the authority to raise and maintain a standing army, therefore it could not expel the British from the forts along the northern frontier that they continued to occupy illegally, in violation of the peace treaty. In addition to these failures, Congress was unable adequately to deal with conflicts between states, a task the Privy Council had performed prior to independence.

Even before the formal ratification of the Articles of Confederation in March 1781, there was agitation for amendment, although relatively few political leaders felt there was any urgency about such proposals. As would be the case for many years, most political decisions that had direct impact on Americans were made by state or local governments. Because the most important decisions were being made closer to home and because travel was both dangerous and expensive, men were unwilling to serve in the national capital and Congress had a great deal of trouble assembling a quorum to do business of any sort. When a quorum did appear, there was usually more pressing business at hand than attempting to rewrite the constitution. For instance, there was a long delay before Congress could assemble a quorum to ratify the peace treaty with Great Britain in 1783. There was also some feeling that it would be bad for the country to change the Articles of Confederation and Perpetual Union when they had only been in operation for a brief period; it would make the American government look unstable if the nation could not continue under one constitution for more than a few years.

It was the attempts by individual states to deal with problems between them outside the mechanism provided by Congress that led eventually to the drafting of the new Constitution that supplanted the Articles of Confederation. During the Confederation years, local meetings between two or more states were called fairly frequently. They were a continuation of the earlier impulse to form local confederations under the British Empire. Congress did not approve of such meetings. As one member expressed it, these local conventions had "the appearance of young Congresses."[8] They detracted from Congress's prestige by emphasizing its inability to deal with some particular problem and dealing with it themselves. But the local conventions were necessary—in some cases disputes were otherwise being resolved by violence—and eight or ten were held in the Confederation years. Actually no one was very happy with them. Besides making Congress look even weaker than it actually was, the conventions, because they focused on local issues, tended to divide the union along sectional lines. Indeed, in a strict sense, the meetings were unconstitutional; the Articles of Confederation specifically forbade treaties or alliances between the states unless these were approved by Congress.

The meeting that began the series of events that culminated in the Constitutional Convention of 1787 was one of the unconstitutional sectional conventions just described. The subject was the Potomac River, the boundary between Virginia and Maryland and site of the so-called "Oyster War"—a dispute over dredging for oysters that has continued to claim casualties into the present century. In 1785, the two states attempted to resolve the oyster problem (and related disputes between fishermen and clam diggers) and also to settle some commercial issues: the location and operation of lighthouses, the designation of ports of entry and customs inspections and rules of navigation.

The governor of Maryland proposed the meeting and the Virginia Assembly named four men to meet with representatives from Maryland in Alexandria, Virginia in March, 1785. George Mason, Edmund Randolph, Alexander Henderson, and James Madison were instructed to "frame such liberal and equitable regulations...as may be mutually advantageous."[9] Governor Patrick Henry was supposed to convey these instructions to the delegates, but did not get around to it, and as a result the meeting was very hastily organized and only two of the appointed delegates attended. George Mason learned only by chance that he was expected to attend. As he wrote to James Madison afterwards, "I shou'd not have known that I was one of the Persons appointed, had I not, by mere Accident two or three Days before the Meeting, been informed of it, by two of the Maryland Commissioners writing to me, that they shou'd endeavour to take my House in their Way, and go with me to Alexandria."[10] To relieve some of the awkwardness, George Washington, Mason's friend and neighbor, was hastily enlisted to fill in, joining Mason and Alexander Henderson who was already in Alexandria. They waited several days for the other Virginia delegates to show up, but when a letter from Randolph to Mason on another subject showed that he had no idea he was supposed to come to Alexandria, the group concluded no one else was going to arrive. Washington recalled that at an earlier convention Virginia had held with Pennsylvania, any two commissioners had been authorized to act for the state. He suggested the group follow that precedent, and then graciously invited them to hold their meeting at his home at Mount Vernon. On Thursday March 24, 1785, Washington sent his carriage to Alexandria to pick up George Mason who arrived at Mount Vernon late that afternoon. The other gentlemen arrived the following afternoon and over the weekend completed their business.[11]

The Mount Vernon Compact was a twelve-point agreement covering navigation, port duties, fishing rights, safety measures, and jurisdiction over trials for violations of commercial regulations, piracy, or other crimes committed on the waters of the Potomac, the Pokomoke, and the lower Chesapeake Bay. The delegates also drafted a joint address for their states to send to the president of the Pennsylvania Council, describing their plans to extend navigation of the Potomac further west and to establish a road from the head of navigation to the waters running into the Ohio and asking for Pennsylvania's cooperation.

The Maryland Assembly was pleased with the results of the Mount Vernon Convention and ratified the compact unanimously. They immediately notified Delaware of what they had worked out with Virginia and proposed that a similar agreement now be negotiated between Maryland and Delaware to govern the upper Chesapeake Bay. They also urged Maryland to make formal application to Congress for even more extensive negotiations with Virginia—an interstate compact for agreement on the value of foreign gold and silver coins passing between the two states, for a schedule of duties on imports and exports, for legal procedures affecting commercial contracts and even for a military treaty involving naval protection.

There was a bit of awkwardness, however, on the Virginia side since neither of the official delegates had fully understood their instructions. It turned out that the Virginia Assembly had stipulated that three commissioners—not two—must agree to make a compact and that the agreement was to have been confined to the Potomac and not to other neighboring waters. George Mason complained that "This blundering Business...will give me Trouble & Expence of a Journey to Richmond, next Session, to appologize [sic] for, & explain our Conduct."[12] Fortunately, James Madison managed matters in Richmond and the Mount Vernon Convention was approved before the end of the year.

Like Maryland, Virginia was so pleased with the results of their latest foray into interstate diplomacy that they wished to extend it further. Just before adjourning, in January 1786, the Virginia House authorized Governor Henry to call for a gathering of all the states of the Confederation to meet at Annapolis to "take into consideration the Trade of the UNITED STATES to examine the relative Situations and Trade of the said States to consider how far an uniform System in their commercial Regulations may be necessary to their common Interest and their permanent Harmony." The date set was September 11, 1786; no mention was made of asking permission of Congress.

And so yet another unconstitutional convention was called, and not everyone was pleased. One of Madison's correspondents observed that "the measure appeared...to have a tendency to weaken the authority of Congress, on which the *Union*, & consequently the Liberty and safety of all the States depend."[13] It was bad enough when extra-Congressional treaties were made which dealt merely with local issues, but the Annapolis Convention had a far broader charge and he believed that "all matters of a general tendency, shou'd be in the representative Body of the whole, or under its authority." But Madison believed, as he wrote to Thomas Jefferson, that some good could come of the proposed commercial convention by making it "subservient to a plenipotentiary Convention for amending the Confederation,"[14] that is, by devoting the meeting to preparations for a second general meeting rather than to a discussion of commercial regulations.

That, indeed, was what occurred. On the day appointed for the Annapolis Convention to begin its deliberations, only three states were present officially. Virginia, Delaware, and New Jersey had sent full delegations and could therefore cast binding votes for their states. One man arrived from Pennsylvania, and two from New York. No one was present to represent Maryland or the seven other states.

Attendance might have improved had the convention been willing to wait. Given the problems of travel and the impossibility of notifying those waiting when some accident or illness caused delay, official bodies were accustomed to long waits for a quorum to assemble. But the scanty attendance worked to the interest of those who wished to avoid the discussion of commercial matters and use the convention merely as a preliminary to a convention with broader powers. At any rate, the Annapolis Convention began its meetings promptly on September 11, 1786, decided the same day that it would "be inexpedient for this Convention, in which so few States are represented, to proceed in the business committed to them;"[15] and three days later they had adopted a report and were ready to adjourn.

The report of the Annapolis Convention was the work of Alexander Hamilton of New York. It was directed to the legislatures of the five states that had representatives present, and, "from motives of respect," the convention sent copies of the report to the legislatures of the other eight states and to Congress. After explaining that the delegates felt they could not "proceed upon the business of their Mission" because of the "partial and defective" representation, the report made a passing reference to that "business," the power to regulate trade, observing that any attempt to deal with the subject would probably "require a correspondent adjustment of other Parts of the Foederal System." Then the commissioners expressed "their unanimous conviction" that every state in the Confederation should appoint commissioners to meet in Philadelphia on the second Monday of the following May in order "to take into Consideration the situation of the United States, to devise such further Provisions as shall appear to them necessary to render the Constitution of the Foederal Government adequate to the exigencies of the Union; and to report such an Act for that purpose to the United States in Congress Assembled." They recommended that Congress treat the report of the Philadelphia convention as suggested amendments to the Articles of Confederation, which, when "agreed to by them and afterwards confirmed by the Legislatures of every State," would become part of the Articles of Confederation.[16]

The Annapolis report was something of an embarrassment to Congress, and although it was received on September 20, 1786, it was not acted upon for four months. The delay resulted from a disagreement between those who endorsed the Annapolis report and those who felt that an amending convention originating with any body other than Congress would be unconstitutional. Those who held the second view wished some state to instruct its delegates in Congress to call for a Congressionally sponsored convention in place of that called by the men at Annapolis. In mid-February, the New York Legislature issued such instructions and Congress adopted a resolution stating "that in the opinion of Congress it is expedient that on the second Monday in May next a Convention of delegates who shall have been appointed by the several States be held at Philadelphia for the sole and express purpose of revising the Articles of Confederation and reporting to Congress and the several Legislatures such alterations and provisions therein as shall when agreed to in Congress and confirmed by the States render the federal Constitution adequate to the exigencies of Government and the preservation of the Union."[17] In other words, the Congress called for a convention to meet under its auspices at exactly the same time and place as the convention called by the Annapolis Convention. By this time five states had chosen delegates to go to Philadelphia and after Congress passed its resolution, six other states made appointments. New Hampshire finally got around to appointing delegates in June, a month after the Convention was to begin, and the state of Rhode Island refused to recognize the convention at all. Rhode Island had a reputation for carrying the Whig suspicion of all government to extremes.

And so the Constitutional Convention met at Philadelphia in the summer of 1787 with representatives of only 12 of the 13 states present. Since all thirteen states must approve amendments to the Articles of Confederation, this did not look very promising. But the delegates proceeded with their work anyway. Some of them, in fact, had done some serious caucusing ahead of time.

On the date the Convention was supposed to begin, Monday, May 14, 1787, only Pennsylvania and Virginia had delegates present. It had been raining hard the week before and the roads were deep in mud. Not until May 25th did a quorum of seven states have representatives present. By that time those delegates who were most devoted to the thorough revision and strengthening of the central government had prepared a draft for a totally new constitution. It was introduced in the Convention by Edmund Randolph of Virginia, and this draft became the basis of all subsequent discussions.

The document released when the Philadelphia Convention adjourned in September 1787 shocked many people. The meetings had been secret, but everyone assumed that what the Philadelphia Convention was working on was amendments to the Articles of Confederation. During its meetings it was not known as a Constitutional Convention; that title came later. At the time it was simply known as the Federal Convention or the Grand Convention. What was released, however, was not a set of amendments but an entirely new constitution. Furthermore, the provisions made for ratification in Article VII were unconstitutional under the established Articles of Confederation, and worse yet, the Constitution contained no bill of rights. The absence of a bill of rights seemed so shocking an omission that three delegates in the convention itself—including Edmund Randolph, who had proposed the original draft constitution, and George Mason—refused to sign it. In 1776, Mason had drafted the Virginia Declaration of Rights which reflected generally accepted Whig principles, and he did not see how a government which refused to guarantee basic individual liberties could be proposed to a free people.

Article VII of the federal Constitution was revolutionary. According to the Articles of Confederation, amendments could be made only if these were first approved by the Continental Congress and then by the legislatures of all the states. Article VII of the proposed federal Constitution did not mention the Continental Congress at all. It declared that the old union would be dissolved as soon as nine of the thirteen states ratified the new Constitution. For those who valued the union of the states—which meant virtually all Americans—this was a frightening prospect. Perhaps the union could do without the state of Rhode Island, but what would happen if the states of New York and Virginia refused to ratify? For many months it appeared that they would refuse.

The proposed federal Constitution gave the central government of the United States far more power than had been given to it under the Articles of Confederation. Most people were not too concerned about the increased powers to regulate trade. After all, most Americans were not involved in commerce. They were farmers whose trade was barter with neighbors. What did concern them was the power to levy direct taxes combined with the power to raise a national army. That combination of the power of the purse and the power of the sword was what had led to tyranny under the Stuart kings and more recently under George III. That was the kind of power which, when misused, led to ordinary citizens getting killed. The absence of a bill of rights made this surrender of power to the central government even more frightening. Had the Constitution been submitted to a popular referendum, it would have been decisively defeated.

Article VII of the proposed Constitution, however, did not ask for a popular vote. It did not ask for approval by state legislatures—which were popularly elected—either. It asked for approval by ratifying conventions specially chosen for this single purpose. But even these conventions refused to accept the proposed Constitution as it came from the Philadelphia Convention; the majority insisted that more protection for individual liberties was needed before the Constitution was acceptable and attached lists of proposed amendments to their acts of ratification. In particular, they were concerned that a specific statement be included that all powers not specifically delegated to the central government would be reserved to the states or to the people. This eventually became the tenth of the first ten amendments.

The action of the Constitutional Convention could have destroyed the American union. Indeed, when George Washington was inaugurated as President of the United States in 1789, the union no longer had thirteen states. Rhode Island and North Carolina refused to come in until the First Federal Congress chosen under the Constitution had actually adopted the Bill of Rights and submitted it to the states for ratification. Only then would the two hold–outs rejoin the union which, they had been arguing, had actually seceded from them by abandoning the Articles of Confederation and Perpetual Union.

Many old patriots, however, including George Mason, were not satisfied with the Bill of Rights voted by Congress even though the first eight of the ten amendments can be traced directly to the

Virginia Bill of Rights, which Mason had drafted in 1776. The Congressional package, introduced by James Madison, had been assembled very carefully, omitting controversial topics for which it might be difficult to muster legislative majorities in the states. However, those who accepted traditional Whig political theory, as most old Patriots did, would not find Madison's amendments sufficient to prevent the system established by the Constitution from degenerating into tyranny. "Some valuable rights are indeed declared," wrote Richard Henry Lee, "but the power to violate them to all intents and purposes remains unchanged."[18] George Mason described the Madison package as mere "Milk & Water Propositions...by way of th[r]owing out a Tub to the Whale."[19]

The unfriendly reception Madison's amendments received from Mason and other Antifederalists led many to believe, both then and later, that the opposition to the Constitution had never been sincere in its demand for a bill of rights, but had used that objection simply as a cover for less admirable doctrines. Supporters of the Constitution tended to consider Antifederalist objections to the Constitution as of two types: the first set demanded more explicit protections of individual rights—freedom of religion, freedom of the press, and so on—and these were generally viewed as appropriate even when the sincerity of the Antifederalists themselves was questioned. The second set sought changes in the structure of the government in order to prevent it from becoming a threat to individual rights. Federalists viewed these proposals with apprehension, fearing they would excessively weaken the new government. But to the Antifederalists the alterations they were suggesting were needed to deprive it of the power to do what would be verbally forbidden by a Bill of Rights. Structural alterations were seen as an indispensable supplement to the amendments dealing with personal liberty.

The Antifederalists' structural objections to the Constitution derived from their adherence to orthodox doctrines of political science that had been accepted as axiomatic in America since before the Revolution. The willingness of so many political leaders to abandon the traditional principles and to trust their liberty to the verbal abstractions of an untried Constitution astonished those Antifederalists who were sensitive to ideological issues. "So wonderfully are mens minds now changed upon the subject of liberty," Richard Henry Lee of Virginia wrote to Samuel Adams of Massachusetts, "that it would seem as if the sentiments universally prevailed in 1774 were antediluvian visions, and not the solid reason of fifteen years ago."[20]

The minds of certain of the old patriots, particularly those of Virginia, had been, as historian Bernard Bailyn expresses it, patterned by a "peculiar configuration of ideas" which "constituted in effect an intellectual switchboard wired so that certain combinations of events would activate a distinct set of signals—danger signals, indicating hidden impulses and the likely trajectory of events impelled by them."[21] In particular, four traditional axioms were contradicted by the form of the new Constitution.

The first of these axioms stated that failure to maintain vigorous State governments would inevitably lead to tyranny, a doctrine usually associated with the French writer Montesquieu. "The most essential danger from the present system arises, in my opinion," wrote Richard Henry Lee, "from its tendency to a consolidated government, instead of a union of Confederated States. The history of the world and reason concur in proving, that so extensive a territory as the United States comprehend, never was, or can be, governed in freedom under the former idea...."[22] Nor can this reasoning be easily faulted. The men of 1789 could hardly have been expected to foresee the transportation revolution which effectively shrank the size of the United States, or the adoption of the Fourteenth Amendment which made the federal government a more effective protector of individual rights than state governments.

That the Constitution was, in fact, intended to produce a consolidated government, was proven to the Antifederalists by its violation of a second axiom of sound politics, namely the danger of placing the powers of purse and sword in the same hands. The power to tax was granted by Article I, Section 8, and it was placed in the control of the central legislature, which, according to the dicta of Revolutionary War days, was too remote from the people to be trusted with so vital a power. Was it not over precisely this issue that America had separated from England? But still worse, this same Congress, by Article I, Section 8, had the power to raise and maintain an army and navy and also to assume command of State militia units.

A third point at which the Constitution defied accepted political doctrine was in what appeared to be a "dangerous blending of the Legislative and Executive powers" that would destroy the balance which Constitutional theorists had praised as the source of English political and civil liberty. "It has hitherto been supposed a fundamental truth," wrote Richard Henry Lee, "that in governments rightly balanced, the different branches of legislature should be unconnected, and that the legislative and executive powers should be separate. In the new constitution, the president and senate have all the executive and two-thirds of the legislative; and in some weighty instances (as making all kinds of treaties which are to be the law of the land) they have the whole legislative and executive powers."[23]

The vast powers of the president, in particular, aroused the apprehensions of men conditioned to fear executive authority. As the legal historian Charles Warren pointed out many years ago, the Philadelphia Convention agreed to most of the presidential powers at a point in their proceedings when the president was to be elected by the Congress and ineligible for reelection. These restrictions were removed in the final days of the Convention and thus created an executive far more powerful than had been originally intended.[24]

Federalists tried to answer the last objection by arguing that George Washington, who would surely be the first elected president, could not conceivably abuse the power granted him and become a tyrant. By arguing this they violated a fourth canon of the traditional political faith: power corrupts, "it having been found from universal experience that the most express declarations and reservations are necessary to protect the just rights and liberty of Mankind, from the silent, powerful, and ever active conspiracy of those who govern," to quote Richard Henry Lee again.[25] Energetic government was not evil in itself—indeed even Antifederalists admitted that more energy in central administration was desirable for America—but care had to be taken to balance power with power, to delegate it cautiously and with ample structural limitations or the natural human tendency to abuse power would inevitably corrupt the system and individual liberty would be the casualty.

Those who accepted these traditional views would not find Madison's amendments sufficient to prevent the system established by the Constitution from degenerating into tyranny. "Some valuable rights are indeed declared," wrote Richard Henry Lee, "but the power to violate them to all intents and purposes remains unchanged."[26]

But Whig arguments were abstract. Most Americans who had felt uneasy about the new Constitution were satisfied by Madison's amendments. An Antifederalist from Maine wrote to his future Congressman, "You laugh at a Bill of Rights; but should one ever be annexed to the Constitution, I will fall down and worship it."[27] After holding out for two years, Virginia passed the decisive act of ratification on 15 December 1791 and the Bill of Rights became part of the Constitution. Though unwilling to worship it, George Mason bowed to political reality.

Worship, however, is probably not too strong a word to describe the attitude of many Americans to the Constitution once amended. Indeed, some came to worship it more devotedly than the Union itself. In the nineteenth century, strict-Constructionists appealing to the Constitution, rather than to abstract principles of political theory, defended nullification and ultimately secession. How would the Founding Fathers have felt about that? Most likely, they would have been unhappy, but not surprised, to find that the instrument designed to form a more perfect Union had produced a Union that was still less than perfect. After all, it was the diversity in American society that made union so important to begin with. And on the merits of the nullification and secession arguments? The Founding Fathers, who battled vigorously among themselves through every step of the constitution-making process and never did achieve consensus, would again have been divided.

Notes

1. Quoted in Edmund Morgan, *The Birth of the Republic, 1763–1789* (Chicago: University of Chicago Press, 1956), 7.

2. Robert A. Rutland, ed., *The Papers of George Mason, 1725–1792*, 3 vols. (Chapel Hill: University of North Carolina Press, 1971), 3:1001.

3. Quoted in Linda Grant De Pauw, *Four Traditions: Women of New York During the American Revolution* (Albany: N.Y.S. American Revolution Bicentennial Commission, 1974), 9.

4. Ibid.

5. *Diary and Autobiography of John Adams*, ed. L. H. Butterfield (Cambridge: Harvard University Press, 1961), 2:109.

6. J. Hector St. John De Crèvecoeur, *Letters from an American Farmer* (New York: E. P. Dutton & Co., 1957), 39.

7. Linda Grant De Pauw, "Land of the Unfree: Legal Limitations on Liberty in Pre-Revolutionary America," *Maryland Historical Magazine* 68 (1973): 368.

8. Quoted in Linda Grant De Pauw, *The Eleventh Pillar* (Ithaca: Cornell University Press, 1966), 45.

9. Helen Hill Miller, *George Mason: Gentleman Revolutionary* (Chapel Hill: University of North Carolina Press, 1975), 229.

10. Rutland, *Papers of George Mason*, 2:826.

11. Miller, *George Mason*, 229–230.

12. Rutland, *Papers of George Mason*, 2:827.

13. United States Bureau of Rolls and Library, *Documentary History of the Constitution of the United States of America, 1787–1870*, 5 vols. (Washington: Dept. of State, 1894–1903), 4:6.

14. Ibid., 21.

15. Egbert Benson's Minutes of the Annapolis Convention, Emmet Collection, #9398–9399, New York Public Library.

16. Documentary History, *1:1–5.*

17. Worthington C. Ford and Gaillard Hunt, eds., *Journals of the Continental Congress, 1774–1789* (Washington: U.S. Government Printing Office, 1904–1937), 32:73–74.

18. James Curtis Ballagh, ed., *The Letters of Richard Henry Lee*, 2 vols. (New York: The Macmillan Co., 1911–14), 2:503.

19. George Mason to John Mason, July 31, 1789, Mason Papers, Library of Congress.

20. Ballagh, *Letters of Richard Henry Lee*, 2:495.

21. Bernard Bailyn, *The Ideological Origins of the American Revolution* (Cambridge, Mass.: Harvard University Press, 1967), 22.

22. Ballagh, *Letters of Richard Henry Lee*, 2:502.

23. Ibid., 2:457–458.

24. Charles Warren, *The Making of the Constitution* (Boston: Little, Brown and Co., 1928), 770.

25. Richard Henry Lee to William Shippen, Jr., October 2, 1787, Shippen Papers, Library of Congress.

26. Ballagh, *Letters of Richard Henry Lee*, 2:503.

27. Thomas B. Waite to George Thacher, August 15, 1788, George Thacher Papers, Boston Public Library.

2

Mason Versus Madison: Developing an American Theory of Federal Democracy

DANIEL J. ELAZAR
Professor of Political Science and Director,
Center for the Study of Federalism, Temple University

Introduction

IN THE EARLY YEARS OF THE CENTER FOR THE STUDY of federalism at Temple University, federalism was an issue which, in *Time* magazine journalese, is known as a M.E.G.O. issue, an acronym for "my eyes glaze over." The *Time* magazine editorial staff proverbially writes M.E.G.O. across dull copy, which then goes into the wastebasket. Today federalism is one of the most important issues of the American political system. Indeed, in our time, it has become one of the most important issues in the political world, throughout the world. Over three-quarters of the human race now live within federal systems or systems utilizing federal arrangements. Yet federalism, however important, is one of those issues which has all too often fallen under the rubric of a subjective M.E.G.O.

I do not have any George Mason stories with which to introduce this paper. The fact that I do not, even though I looked for some, reflects the degree to which George Mason is, if not unsung, at least undersung in American history. Even the great event in which he took part 200 years ago, the Mount Vernon Conference, will probably go quite unrecognized, even though it led to the institution of a process which not only was of crucial importance for the history of the United States of America, but also was of crucial importance for demonstrating that there could be constitutional change through procedures other than violent revolution and abandonment of the principles of democratic republicanism.

As it turns out, George Mason himself was not pleased with the results of that process which he played a major role in initiating, as we shall see. His critique of the results of the 1787 Constitutional Convention, while, in my opinion, ultimately wrong—that is to say, the notion of rejecting the Constitution drafted in 1787 would not have served the American people in good stead—has many important elements that we should keep before us as we move into the third century of the American federal union. There are many elements in that critique which have turned out to be correct. George Mason did have the foresight to see dangers that lay ahead, dangers which to some extent have been realized. Even if we continue to prefer the results that the American people chose, rather than the result which he wished them to choose, we can learn from his critique.

Those of us who study these questions in what I like to think is a sober fashion, have come to the general conclusion that people can learn more from failure than from success. The trouble with success is that nothing succeeds like success and therefore few people really examine why something succeeded. The virtue of failure is not only that nothing fails like failure but by attempting to learn from failure, one can provide direction for future improvements. And so George Mason's failure holds within it, it seems to me, lessons for us all. This makes it particularly appropriate, then, that in a series devoted to the concerns of George Mason, there should be a volume devoted to federalism.

A Federalist Rejection of Federalism

At first glance, George Mason comes down to us in history as the preeminent or one of the preeminent Antifederalists. An Antifederalist? So why do we discuss federalism? We must recall that George Mason was an Antifederalist who was for federalism. He had a different conception of federalism than that which was advocated by those who became known as the Federalists in American history, a self-assumed name, a brilliant stroke of political genius which led them to appropriate a term which had a different meaning in 1787 and make it theirs. So George Mason, who considered himself far more of a federalist than the Federalists, became known as an Antifederalist. Understanding the fact that George Mason saw himself as a federalist, that his critique was not against federalism but against the kind of constitution which he saw as undermining federalism, makes it very important for us not only to understand his critique, which I already suggested was important, but to understand something about federalism by virtue of the fact that he could consider himself legitimately a federalist as much as the Federalists.

George Mason was a federalist who opposed federation, which is the technical term for what the Constitution of 1787 proposed and succeeded in introducing into the American political system. He was for confederation, another technical term, which we know from the Articles of Confederation. The difference, in a word, is that in a confederation the constituent states create a limited general government which is strictly their creature and which operates only through them to reach the citizens of the confederation who are, first and foremost, citizens of their states and only secondarily citizens of the whole. In a federation, a device invented in its modern form by the framers of the Constitution of 1787, the people are generally citizens of both the general and constituent polities and both the federal government and the constituent governments have spheres of power of their own, through which they are empowered to touch directly the lives of their citizens. Today all

Americans are citizens of the United States *and* of the states in which they reside. That is characteristic of a federation and is what, in the last analysis, gives the federal government a basis for becoming very powerful. Whereas, had George Mason had it his way, the Americans of today would have been citizens of the states in which they reside and through those states, citizens of the United States.

Now George Mason rejected federation for federalist reasons. He thought that federation would provide too much of a consolidation of government—that it would create too strong a government, covering too large a territory to preserve what he understood to be proper republican government and the attendant political and civil rights of the citizens. In suggesting that confederation was a proper form of federalism, he suggested that federalism was not simply what we take it for granted as being in the United States today. Americans today equate federalism with the United States. Of course, America has one kind of federalism, a federation. It may even be the best kind, but it is not the only kind.

As I noted earlier, the Federalists made a brilliant sleight of hand. When George Mason first raised his objections to the Constitution of 1787, the term federal was synonymous with the term confederation or confederal. Indeed, in *The Federalist*, Madison had to refer to the new government being proposed as "partly federal and partly national"—national meaning consolidated—because he was speaking to an audience for whom the term federal meant what we today would term confederal. However, the Federalists knew that Americans were committed to federalism and to the federal principle. Whatever union was formed would have to be based upon some variety of federalism, so the Federalists seized the term for themselves. They took this creature that they invented, which they refer to elsewhere in *The Federalist* as a compound republic—in other words, compounded of constituent units—and they gave it a name, and the name they gave it was "federal." Therefore, those who supported confederation, not having taken that high ground first, were left with the appellation

"Antifederalist." So poor George Mason has come down in history to us as if he were opposed to federalism.

What is Federalism?

In fact, what this suggests to me is that federalism, to use a biological analogy, is a genus composed of several species. Federation is one such species. That is what we have today in the United States. Confederation is another species. I could list a number of others, but space prevents me from doing so. Today there are actually six or seven different species of federalism functioning in the world.

Conventional accounts of American history treat confederation and federation as two very different ways of dealing with the problem of political organization. Indeed, within the limited context of American history, this approach can be understood as reflecting the sense of profound transformation brought about by the U.S. Constitution of 1787. In a larger sense, however, the American experience shows federation and confederation to be two species of the same genus—federalism, each seeking in its own way to combine liberty with appropriately effective government.

If there are these different species of federalism, we should know something about what they have in common—what differentiates them from other forms or genera of government as well as what differentiates them from one another. I have already summarized the basic difference between federation and confederation. I could point out similar differences between each of them and the other species. But what do they have in common? Here is where understanding something about federal theory will help us understand something about our own system of government, how it functions today, and why it functions the way it does. When we find out what it is that federation and confederation and the other species of federalism share, we will understand what is the essence of federalism and what each species must preserve and translate into the realities of everyday political and governmental life if we are to achieve the goals for which federalism was designed. George Mason certainly was committed to those goals, even though he argued for a different path to attaining those goals. Moreover, he was committed to understanding the theory behind those goals because without the theory, it would be impossible to understand the goals themselves.

In a word, federalism has to do with the combination of self-rule and shared rule. At one and the same time it involves the combination of political entities that desire to continue to rule themselves but also desire to share in an enduring political community. That is true even if we are talking about the classic political idea that all civil society is federal, that is to say, is constituted by its members who have covenanted or compacted with each other to form a body politic while preserving their respective integrities as individuals, so that they rule themselves while at the same time being part of civil society and functioning together in such a way that collectively they share rule with each other. It is this particular characteristic which lies at the root of any theory of federalism. Any theory that purports to be federal which does not relate to this effort to combine self-rule and shared rule is fallacious or inadequate.

To some extent this aspect of federalism is a little bit like trying to have one's cake and eating it too. Indeed, federalism relates to that great human desire of trying to do just that. The late Martin Diamond used to give what he called the Jimmy Durante definition of federalism. In the movie classic *The Man Who Came To Dinner*, Durante comes to visit the central figure in the movie, Sheridan Whiteside, the man who has broken his leg on the doorstep of his quasi-friends in a small midwestern town. In his madcap way, Durante sits down at the piano and starts to bang out a song whose opening line is "Did you ever have the feeling that you wanta go and the feeling that you wanta stay?" That is federalism; on one hand you want to go, to be independent. On the other hand, you want to stay, you want to be part of something larger than yourself.

An additional element in any federal theory is that federalism involves non–centralization, that is to say, it involves multiple centers of authority and power which are held together through some constitutional vehicle which constitutionalizes non–centralization. A final element of any theory of federalism is that authority is to be divided while power is to be shared. Again, that is an aspect of self–rule and shared rule.

Federalism, then, I am suggesting, has to do primarily with relationships and only secondarily with structures. Because of what happened in the 19th century—discussions of American federalism surrounding slavery, states' rights, secession, and segregation in which the Commonwealth of Virginia took the lead—when federalism was reduced to a careful and almost hairsplitting analysis of what was legally possible under the United States Constitution and what was not, Americans became preoccupied with federalism as structure.

The Confederalist Argument and the Federalist Response

The issues of what constitutes the legitimate exercise of federal power and what is a legitimate exercise of state power, are important questions. I do not mean to diminish or denigrate them. But treated in the way they were then, they soon become questions that remain at the level of structural considerations. Structure is very important but structure is important as a way of expressing relationships, not for its own sake.

George Mason was fearful of the proposed federal Constitution because he thought it would so change the relationship between the states and the federal government and establish so problematic a relationship between the federal government and the individuals who composed the American people, that it would reduce liberty. His opponents argued that it is precisely this change in relationships that was necessary if liberty were to survive. James Madison, Mason's Northern Virginia neighbor and his great opponent on this issue, argued that only in an extended republic where the pettiness of individual states is somehow moderated by the multiplicity of interests that come together under a federal framework, will liberty be preserved. Mason's position was that the creation of such an extended republic would rob the small republics of their power to foster community and without community, liberty cannot be preserved. This historic debate has continued as a perennial debate about relationships and about the structures that flow from relationships. It is a debate, I would submit, about federal democracy.

As we commemorate the 200th anniversary of the completion of the adoption of the Articles of Confederation, it behooves Americans and students of politics everywhere to reexamine the American experience under confederation as well as federation, and most especially the principles underlying the confederal experiment, to try to understand exactly how both species of the same genus were given their modern form in the new United States. Such a reexamination is especially appropriate at this time because the serious revival of confederal options around the world since World War II inevitably leads us back to the original American experience. In the century following adoption of the Articles of Confederation, there were other confederal experiments in Europe and Latin America, all of which foundered in the face of the nationalistic tendencies of the modern epoch which emphasized the linkage of nation–building and state–building on a centralized basis or, at a minimum, along the lines of federation. In the post–modern epoch, on the other hand, constitutionalized transnational political organization based on shared economic and cultural foundations has been more acceptable, leading to a renewed interest in the possibilities of confederation.

The modern character of the American confederation and its connection with federalism are important to note at the outset. One of the reasons for ignoring the close relationship between the confederal and federal experiences of the American confederation is that students have treated it as if it were simply a late example of a pre–modern league rather than a perpetual union of states. Indeed this view was developed directly and explicitly by the authors of *The Federalist* as part of their polemic against the Articles of Confederation and on behalf of the new federal Constitution. One can understand their reasons for trying to identify the existing confederation with the ancient and medieval European leagues which were pre–modern expressions of the federal principle. However, it behooves us to question the accuracy of what they did. Their descriptions of the weaknesses of those leagues are generally accurate, and their attribution of some of those self–same weaknesses to the American confederation was also justified; but in the heat of the political battle, they went beyond that. Whether they properly classified the American confederation with those leagues needs to be examined more closely.

The polity established by the Articles was a "Confederation and Perpetual Union" as described in its preamble, while the Constitution of 1787 was designed to "form a more perfect Union." Therein lie the similarity and the difference. The confederation established by the Articles was perpetual and had virtually unlimited power within its sphere. It was far more than an alliance since, when a state acceded to it, it could no more withdraw than can a state from the federal union. Moreover, in international law, the United States of America was an independent entity constituted by its states and not simply a committee of them. It was a confederacy (Article 1) which came into existence only after ratification by all of the member states. Were it merely a treaty or alliance, it could have come into existence for those states ratifying it immediately upon their ratification. In fact, it hardly can be said to have "come into existence" because, in reality, the Articles represented a formal constitutionalization of what had been established in 1775 by "the United States in Congress assembled," an entity which continued to function from 1775 to 1781 even while the Articles were pending ratification.

Here I will suggest that confederation and federation as developed in the United States after 1775 were both modern devices. As such, American style confederation, no less than federation, was a different form of political organization from the earlier leagues. That is one reason why the study of the American confederal experience does not lead us away from federalism, but improves our understanding of federalism as a genus whose principles and arrangements are applicable in the real world.

What Constitutes Liberty?

The central interest of both federation and confederation and, indeed, of true federalism in all its species, is the issue of liberty. All forms of federalism begin with the assumption that government in some form is necessary and that the development of appropriately effective government is a major human task. In this respect, federalist theories are realistic. The other "given" of federalism is that humans are born free and that good government must be grounded in a framework of maximum human liberty. The task of constitution makers is to develop a regime for their people which secures liberty while recognizing and allowing for government in its coercive aspects.

To say that liberty stands at the center of federalist striving is to open the door to the question of what constitutes liberty in the federal context and how federalists deal with the problematics of liberty. On one level, these questions lead to what may be the decisive difference between confederation and federation. Federations are communities of both polities and individuals, and emphasize the liberties of both. The American federation has placed even greater emphasis on the liberty of individuals than on the liberties of its constituent polities, an emphasis which has grown more pronounced over the generations.

Confederations, on the other hand, are primarily communities of polities, which place greater emphasis on the liberties of the constituent polities. It is the task of the constituent polities to protect individual liberty, more or less as each defines it, although the constituent polities of confederation in republics must conform to at least minimum standards of individual liberty in order to preserve the republican character of the whole. The minimum guarantee of individual liberty in the Articles can be found in Article IV, which gave the "free inhabitants in each of these states...all privileges and immunities of free citizens in the several states... free ingress and regress to and from any other state, and...all the privileges of trade and commerce"— in other words, basic civil and commercial rights.

Thus, to understand a confederation, it is necessary, first and foremost, to know what constitutes the liberties of its constituents and how those constituents see confederation as protecting those liberties. American pluralism has stayed far from the concept of group liberties to become almost exclusively individualistic in character. This is not surprising, given the character of American society. No doubt, one of the reasons why it was possible to convince a majority of Americans voting by states to abandon confederation for federation was because, even in the Revolutionary era, the states were not able to command a level of identification stronger than that of individual self-interest because of the growing common perception that Americans were Americans, first and foremost.

Had the states been perceived by a majority of their citizens to be primary organic communities as George Mason argued, there is little doubt that the Constitution of 1787 would have been rejected on behalf of state liberties. As it was, the real challenge to that document revolved around the protection of individual liberty (i.e., the need for a bill of rights in the federal Constitution). Not that the principle of state liberties was totally rejected—the political liberties of the states were deemed to be very important, as witness the Tenth Amendment—but they were not primary in the American scheme of things.

Because of this special character of American pluralism, Americans have a very difficult time understanding issues of group rights. That made federation easy for them, but for much of the world, group rights—variously defined as national, local, or ethnic liberties—are of the essence. For these people, confederation may be the most viable way to attain the combination of liberty, good government, and peace which federalism promises.

On another level, both species of federalism must deal with the perennial problematics of liberty. Whether articulated or not (and in the United States, it usually is not), the foundation of this issue rests on the distinction between natural liberty and federal liberty. Natural liberty is unrestricted, the freedom of the state of nature, whether understood in Hobbesian or Lockean terms. In the end, it is the liberty that leads to anarchy, or the war of all against all. According to federal principles, proper liberty is federal liberty, that is, the liberty to act according to the terms of the covenant (*foedus*) which calls the body politic into existence. Every proper polity is established by a pact among its constituents which is covenantal insofar as it rests upon a shared moral sensibilty and understanding and is legitimate insofar as it embodies the fundamental principles of human liberty and equality. Behavior which does not fall within those terms is, in effect, a violation of the covenant and a manifestation of anarchy. Hence, it can be stopped and its perpetrators punished by the appropriate institutions of government.

In sum, federal liberty is liberty established by agreement. The content of any particular agreement may and will vary. Thus, John Winthrop could understand true liberty as that flowing from the covenant between God and man in which God dictated the terms of the agreement and which man pledged to accept. On the other hand, James Wilson of Pennsylvania, one of the authors of the Constitution of 1787, could understand federal liberty as a strictly secular expression of the compact establishing civil society. Today, when the Supreme Court of the United States holds the state and federal governments to standards of behavior based upon the United States Constitution, even when the implementation of those standards places heavy restrictions on individual behavior, in effect, it does so on the grounds that the Constitution is a compact entered into by the people of the United States which, *inter alia*, delineates what constitutes federal liberty within the American system.

This discussion would not be complete if we did not recall that one of the basic tensions which informs American civilization is the tension between natural and federal liberty. Admiration for the former has been expressed in various ways in American history from the eighteenth-century ideal of the "noble savage" to the "natural man" of the nineteenth century, to "doin' what comes naturally" in the first half of the twentieth, to the "let it all hang out" of our times. Indeed, natural liberty was clearly dominant in the land from the mid-1960s through the 1970s.

Federal liberty found its first expression in the theopolitical stance of the Puritans, and has retained favor among those applying religious standards and moral expectations to the American people and their polity—including the eighteenth-century revolutionaries, the anti-slavery forces of the antebellum years, the Populists and Progressives of the late nineteenth century, and those who fought the civil rights battles of the 1950s and 1960s. All of the foregoing believed that people were not naturally free to commit certain wrongs, but, as citizens or residents of the United States, living under its Constitution, could be required to act or refrain from acting according to the terms of that Constitution.

The Articles of Confederation had as the focus of their concern the federal liberty of the constituent states. Hence, they had what was at once a more limited and far broader definition of federal liberty with which to work, restricting the freedom of the constituent states in those few fields where it was deemed necessary for a uniform confederal standard while allowing each in its own way to determine what constituted federal liberty for its own citizens.

Federation and Confederation

Returning to the differences between federation and confederation, we may begin with the classic distinction; namely, that in federations, the federal government can reach out directly to its citizenry as well as through the constituent polities, while in confederation the confederal government must reach individual citizens only through the constituent polities. This definition is accurate as far as it goes, but it is not complete. We must add the point made above that a federation is more concerned with the preservation of individual liberty while a confederation places greater emphasis on the preservation of local liberties of its constituent polities.

A third characteristic distinguishing federations from confederations is that the former have a common law of some scope which is enforceable throughout the federation, while the latter tend to leave matters of law to the constituent polities except as explicitly provided in limited areas determined to be of such general concern that they must be governed by a common law. This is a matter of the greatest importance; some might even say the heart of the matter. Federation is possible only where a sufficiently comprehensive common law binding all citizens of the constituent units is possible. By the same token, confederation is a viable means of establishing federal ties in situations where the parties to the bargain can only tolerate specific and limited common laws.

The Articles provided for a common law of war and peace and a common foreign relations. Implicit in the Articles is a common republicanism which is so taken for granted that it finds expression only in Article VI in the prohibition against granting titles of nobility. The Confederacy also had full powers over coinage, weights and measures, and postal service.

The most ambiguous elements in the Articles are those relating to interstate commerce and the general welfare. On the one hand, it is clear from Article IV that the United States is to be a single entity for commercial purposes, but without eliminating the powers of the states to protect their own respective economies, as suggested obliquely in Article VI. Similarly, there are two references to the general welfare, one in Article III as one of the ends of the Confederacy, and the second in Article VIII with regard to the revenue–raising powers of the new Congress. Both references are general and open–ended.

A fourth dimension must be added, having to do with the ends of the polity. Every polity is devoted to the attainment of certain ends, to the achievement of justice as it is conceived by those who constitute it. In this respect, the extent to which the general government possesses power, while crudely related to the defined ends of the polity, is not determinative of those ends. One of the perceived problems of the American confederation is that the confederal government was not adequate for the achievement of the ends for which it was instituted. We have already mentioned two elements involved in determining the ends of federal polities: namely, liberty, however defined, and good government, however defined. In both cases, federal polities, because they are constituted in a formal way by a pact of articles of agreement, are likely to be more explicit about their understanding of these and other ends to which they are devoted. These ends are generally stated in the preambles to their constitutions, but may also be stated or explicated in the body of the constitutional document(s).

As a general rule, confederations have more limited ends than federations. With respect to the United States, the principal difference between the Constitution of 1787 and the Articles of Confederation was one of means rather than ends. In this aspect, the Preamble to the 1787 Constitution specified that what is proposed is the establishment of "a more perfect union," not a new one. What was changed were the means for effectuating the union, which required the expansion of the powers granted to the federal government even in order to obtain already agreed upon ends.

The major shift with regard to ends was from an emphasis on the liberties of the individual states to the establishment of liberty, justice, and domestic tranquility for the people of the United States. Article III of the Articles sets forth the ends of the Confederation:

> The said states hereby severally enter into a firm league of friendship with each other, for their common defence, the security of their Liberties, and their mutual and general welfare, binding themselves to assist each other,

> against all force offered to, or attacks made upon them, or any of them, on account of religion, sovereignty, trade, or any other pretence whatever.

Contrast it with the Preamble to the Constitution of 1787:

> We the people of the United States, in Order to form a more perfect Union, establish Justice, insure domestic Tranquility, provide for the common defence, promote the general Welfare, and secure the blessings of liberty to ourselves and our Posterity, do ordain and establish this Constitution for the United States of America.

I would not want to minimize this shift. In a certain sense, it is of the essence; but it is not, as some would have it, the exchange of a loose league for a consolidated union. There is more of a shift in emphasis than in underlying form. I do not wish to enter here into the question of how effective or ineffective the Confederation was; that dispute is well–known. One thing is clear, however. While we cannot and never will know whether the potentialities within the Articles of Confederation could have been developed to deal with the problems of a growing United States, the confederal government was not simply a failure.

It had a number of accomplishments, not the least of which involved the extension of its powers into new spheres, whether with regard to the organization of western lands (after all, the Confederation Congress established the basis for the admission of new states into the United States), in banking (the Confederation Congress established the first bank in the United States as its instrumentality), or in the initiation of support for educational and eleemosynary development.

Following Madison, the distinction between the two regimes can be summarized as follows: the Constitution of 1787 provided a government that was partly national and partly federal to replace the Articles of Confederation, which itself had established a regime that was partially federal and partially a league. The first combination came to be known as federation; the second came to be known as confederation. The tension built into the former is between the national and the federal elements, while the tension built into the latter is between the federal elements. Since federal arrangements always involve one or another set of built-in tensions, the character of the tension of each particular arrangement is the major clue as to the species of federalism involved.

The difficulties—often fatal—of confederation flow from this basic tension. In our consideration of whether confederation can be a viable option, we must raise the question as to whether (or under what conditions) the confederal tension can be sustained in a polity on a long-term basis. This is a real issue in the European Community today.

The American Rationale for Confederation

The American Confederacy and the Articles of Confederation which established and guided it must be understood as a Whig mechanism, an extension of the commonwealth principles which informed constitution-making in most, if not all, of the individual states. It has the classic dimension of an Old Whig or Commonwealthman polity, American style. It is covenantal rather than contractual since it relies principally on the states' moral commitment to making the Articles effective for the enforcement of its provisions. It not only required consent but emphasized it in the Whig manner by requiring the constant renewal or reaffirmation of consent at almost every step in the governmental process. In this respect, it relied on another Whig principle, republican virtue, as the mainstay of the polity since it was implicit that only if republican virtue flourished would the states live up to their moral commitment.

The Whig reliance on republican virtue was tied in with emphasis on homogeneous polities in which community would exist to foster republican virtue and a shared public interest. That is one of the major reasons why the United States as a whole could be no more than a confederation in the Whig scheme of things. It was too diverse to properly foster or maintain either republican virtue or shared public interest. (That is why in the debate over the ratification of the Constitution of 1787 the Federalists concentrated their attack on the notion that the states could be sufficiently homogeneous, arguing that they also were too large.) For the Whigs, the states had that capacity, which was another reason why each state was to vote with one voice in the Congress and was to be responsible for implementing (i.e., appropriately adapting) the acts of Congress.

In Whig tradition, the Confederacy's principal institution was the legislature, formally titled "the United States in Congress assembled." It, in turn, was tied as closely as possible to the people or, more accurately, to the polities it represented, following the Whig pattern of exercising control first over governmental power and then over the governors who exercise it. The members of the Congress were delegates chosen and supported by those who sent them, and sat for limited terms only, again a classic Whig control device also found in most of the early state constitutions. There was heavy reliance upon consensual action by several bodies in order to implement programs, particularly the United States in Congress assembled and the individual states, but also Congress and its Executive Committee, with minimum sanctions to bring about cooperation among them and a heavy emphasis upon each accepting its moral responsibilty (or consenting) to do its share.

The practical deficiencies of the Whig approach to governance soon became apparent in the states as well as the Confederacy. A great part of the triumph of the Federalists over the Whigs lay in their genius in creating better mechanisms of governance, through which Whig principles could be embodied in Federalist institutions. Ultimately, it was this synthesis of Whig principles and Federalist institutions that created the golden age of American federalism. We should have learned from the Confederation years and the period since 1865 that, to the extent that one or the other is abandoned, the country suffers, but more on that below.

The existence of the Confederation was taken for granted from the first. There was never any debate as to whether the states should be united. The debate centered around the character of the union, not its existence. For all intents and purposes, the union came into existence no later than 1775; indeed, the very process of declaring independence reflected the degree to which the United States of America already existed. In this sense, the union began with the people of the several states seeing themselves from the first as Americans in certain respects, and as linked to one another as Americans across state lines.

This is another way in which the American Confederation was a Whig confederacy, a confederacy of commonwealths that was to embody commonwealth ideals, not like the European leagues or even the United Netherlands which was a union of provincial oligarchies. There is no question as to the republican and popular character of either the American regime or its constitution. The United States was born free under its first constitution as much as under its second. Indeed, the argument in later years was that it was even born freer under its first than under its second. This is an argument that I do not accept; but it is testimony to the ideals embodied in that first American confederation. In other words, the fundamental principles of American government were established under the Articles; namely, that the United States was to be a commonwealth of commonwealths resting on popular and republican[1] bases, able to function only through the cooperative interaction of its components in a nonhierarchical way and committed to partnership to advance common goals for the general welfare.

The great acts of the Confederal Congress reflected this overall thrust. Those acts included the acquisition of the western lands as the common property of the United States, provision for their settlement and organization as future states of the Confederation, the initiation of a national banking system, the provision of a common defense force, and the negotiation of treaties of peace and alliance with the European powers having interests in North America. These and other acts of the Confederation all involve the application of the aforementioned principles in concrete ways. Their success is attested to by the fact that they were continued or reenacted under the new federal Constitution and continued to provide a basis for American development long after the Confederation gave way to a new regime.

Whig Principles and Federalist Mechanisms

The history of the adoption of the Constitution of 1787 can be examined from the perspective of how the Federalists constructed a stable and lasting extended republic by taking the essence of the Whig rationale and standing it on its head so as to overcome its weaknesses. Cutting through the polemics surrounding the struggle over ratification of the Constitution of 1787, we can begin to understand the degree to which the second United States Constitution represented a supplement to the first, a synthesis of old principles and new practices as well as a departure from the first constitution. While the Constitutional Convention produced a well articulated Federalist theory in contradistinction to the Whig theory, it is important to note that the former was not the exclusive theory of all members of the convention or even of those who were most active in drafting the new Constitution. I am suggesting that, the radical Federalists aside, the theory behind the United States Constitution incorporated certain Whig principles to some degree (we need further research to determine to what degree) while transcending them in the invention of the mechanisms of government for which the Constitution is justly famous.

The two most original elements of Federalist theory are the idea of the extended republic as a means of controlling the evils of class and faction and the idea of the separation of powers as a means of providing energetic yet controlled government. Both were simultaneously extensions and transformations of Whig theory. The Federalist theory of the extended republic followed the confederal precedent of the Whigs but, rather than relying on expectations that shared understanding of the commonwealth in politically homogeneous polities would promote good government, the Federalists realistically recognized the problems of class conflict and factional struggles and sought to control them through the device of a large federal republic which could dilute their intensity. So, too, the principle of dispersing power among various units that must function cooperatively or concurrently was not foreign to the Whigs. The crucial addition of the Federalists was the invention of the tripartite separation of powers based on the presidency as the separate executive branch, a judiciary headed by a supreme court, and a bicameral legislature with one house representing the people and the other states. Those who held Whig principles had little difficulty adjusting to this invention which, as a mechanism, offered clear advantages over the kinds of power–sharing which lay at the root of the Whig system, especially since that earlier division between Congress and the states was incorporated into the new Constitution, albeit on somewhat different terms. Indeed the Whigs had already come to the tripartite division in their own state constitutions.

The matter of the extended republic was somewhat more difficult for the Whigs to assimilate. It represented a greater theoretical departure. The Whig premise was that only where those who held the power of government were subject to direct oversight of the citizenry were they likely to be properly controlled. Each extension of government beyond local control presented its own complications for the Whigs. Governments serving larger arenas had to be fenced in with more restraints, albeit moral restraints more than mechanical ones, beyond the narrow bag of Whig tricks such as selecting representatives for the shortest possible terms of office with maximum possible rotation and bound as closely as possible to those who selected them.

Now here was James Madison turning that theory on its ear and arguing just the reverse: that the extended republic offered greater republican stability, not so much because of better formal divisions, but because it prevented the division of society into two classes, the few creditors and the many debtors, which was the case in small republics since time immemorial. This was an argument to be conjured with precisely because it addressed the great question of liberty which preoccupied the Whigs. To the extent that the Constitution of 1787 was based upon this argument, it did represent a radical change.

For our purposes, the great change wrought by the Constitution of 1787 was to be constitutionalized power and its limits, setting forth clearly the expanded powers of the federal government, but also clearly limiting them through mechanisms and institutions designed to keep a potentially powerful government under control. The federal system had become more national in its thrust but was counterbalanced by becoming more explicitly federal in its organization, in contradistinction to the Articles which were more federal in their thrust but more like a league in the organization they established.

In accomplishing this, the new Constitution moved the American people from a reliance upon convenantal principles—that is, moral obligation as a means of ensuring compliance with agreed upon arrangements—to compactual ones, in which the means of compliance and the penalties for non-compliance were specified and enforceable. To say this is to oversimplify to some extent. But, allowing for that oversimplification, in the main it is the best way to describe the fundamental transformation of principle from the first to the second Constitution.

The claim that the United States is indeed a polity founded by covenant can be sustained only in light of the document itself. The Declaration of Independence was the covenant which established the American people and set forth the basic principles to guide them as a people.[2] The Articles of Confederation must be read in light of the Declaration of Independence since many of the silences or ambiguities in the Articles relate to the widely understood and widely accepted principles of the Declaration. In that respect, it is an operational gloss on the covenant itself and, like it, relies on moral commitment for the enforcement of obligations. Thus, both the Declaration and the Articles make references to the Deity: the first "appealing to the Supreme Judge of the World," and the second recognizing that "the Great Governor of the World" inclined "the hearts of the legislatures" of the respective states "to ratify the said articles of confederation and perpetual union." Both references should be understood as more than piety. As in every covenantal document, they are designed to invoke moral obligation. God is made a witness to the proceedings and to the consent freely given to the result. The Constitution of 1787, on the other hand, is long on sanctions or, more accurately, grants of power to Congress to enforce its terms, but contains no reference to Heaven. It is thoroughly secular in its means and ends, a compact rather than a covenant.

On one level, the failures of the Articles of Confederation attest to the limits of covenants without operative sanctions in human society. Nevertheless, a strong measure of Whiggism survived to help inform the new federal Constitution and direct it toward larger ends than those which the radical Federalists proposed as appropriate for the more perfect union. The Whig influence was felt in somewhat contradictory ways, and not necessarily in ways that met the expectations of the old Whigs of the revolutionary generation, but that is all too often the way of human affairs, and we need not be surprised at that result.

The resurgence of Whig influence came simultaneously with the struggle over ratification which, in one sense of course, the Whigs lost. Fearful of the extensive powers granted the federal government under the new Constitution and unwilling fully to trust procedural devices and intricate mechanisms to restrain federal power, the Whigs insisted on the addition of a Bill of Rights to the new Constitution, which was done as soon as the new government was organized. The idea of a Bill of Rights was classic Whig doctrine, though in the case of the federal Constitution, Whigs seemed to have imbibed Federalist principles by demanding a Bill of Rights that was enforceable and not simply a declaration of principles designed to generate moral obligation on the part of the governors toward the governed, as was the case with the declarations of rights in the state constitutions. Thus, in the adoption of the Bill of Rights itself the new synthesis began to be manifest.

Even more far-reaching was the decision on the part of the Antifederalists, most of whom were Whigs, to accept the new Constitution and actively participate in the organization and administration of the new government. By accepting the results of the struggle over ratification, those who shared Whig principles in one way or the other almost immediately gained substantial power within the new federal government and were able to use that power to interpret the new Constitution in a manner consistent with their Whig ideas.

Perhaps one of the best examples of this was Albert Gallatin's introduction of cooperative federalism as the accepted form of intergovernmental relations in the years of Thomas Jefferson's presidency. Rather than exploit powers granted the federal government to enable it to operate directly within the states in pursuit of federal goals, Gallatin developed ways and means of federal–state cooperation whereby the federal government and the states undertook to implement joint programs. In doing this, Gallatin restored the important Whig control device of cooperative action, albeit within the framework of the federal Constitution, which relied less upon good will than heretofore and more upon latent federal powers. Gallatin's efforts were to influence the course of American government and administration from that time forward.

In short, the adoption of the Constitution of 1787 did not simply substitute Federalist for Whig principles, but created a new tension between the two sets of principles which has played itself out through Federalist institutions and a federal, as distinct from a confederal, regime. That tension remains with us. For the first two generations under the Constitution, the United States resembled a confederation almost as much as it did a federation, as those who espoused a confederal approach shaped a federal Constitution to their ends. In the third generation, those who tried to push the confederal approach too far precipitated a civil war, with the inevitable backlash toward federal union. After the corresponding excesses of Reconstruction, however, the federal balance was restored for two more generations, only to be upset in the direction of centralization once again. It was during those generations that Americans lost sight of the principles of the founding generation, both Federalist and Whig. Both covenantal and compactual theories of the polity were rejected in favor of the then more fashionable organic and evolutionary (Darwinian) theories. Concomitantly, hierarchical views of the state came to replace the idea of the federal commonwealth. Progressives and reactionaries, socialists and capitalists, reformers and stand–patters were swept up by the new styles. Only among the midwestern and western Progressives did the Whig outlook continue to prevail while the Federalist outlook came to be confined to politicians with a stake in the system as it existed.

It was only in the post–World War II generation that we began to rediscover the teachings of the Federalist founders, principally through the work of Martin Diamond, and only toward the end of that generation did we begin to pay attention to the Whig founders. We are still engaged in the latter exploration. Only insofar as we understand the ideas and actions of both sets of founders will we be able to understand the origins of the American federal commonwealth and to steer the ship of state in the right direction.

While the Madisonian position won, the American system that emerged from that confrontation is a federal democracy in which something of George Mason is preserved as well. Indeed, for the first 145 years after the adoption of the Constitution of 1787, Mason often seemed to have won over Madison in fact, if not in theory, as his approach to federalism animated the relationships between the states and the federal government within the formal framework established by James Madison. Why? Because the relationships were more important than the structures.

Different Models of Polity

Some additional elements of federal democracy must also be considered. First of all, federalism is different from decentralization. Today political scientists and others are attracted to mapping all political phenomenon on continua—there is a continuum for everything. Among them is a centralization–decentralization continuum with federalism at one end and a centralized unitary government on the other. Toward the middle are decentralized unitary and centralized federal governments, all on one continuum. I would suggest that this kind of conceptualization is one of the reasons why we are having trouble maintaining federalism in the United States today. When you start with an erroneous model, you get an erroneous result.

Federalism is not the same as decentralization. In a decentralized political system there is a center which decides what is to be centralized and what is to be decentralized; ergo, what is decentralized can be recentralized by decision of the center. Federalism is a model for noncentralization which constitutionally guarantees that there shall be no single center. That is the first principle of federalism. On this, James Madison and George Mason were agreed. The federal government was to be a framing institution, not a single power center. The states were to be the constituents of the federal system, the United States of America—the name is a federal name (we say it so easily we do not stop to think about it)—not the peripheries around the center. The term capital implies the top of the power pyramid or the center of power. Washington was not described as the nation's capital until the twentieth century. It was referred to as the seat of the federal or general government–the latter was the preferred term. There is a great difference between the seat of government which is one place within a network of equal places and a capital which reigns on top or which occupies the center. It is only in the twentieth century that Americans began to talk about Washington as the capital. We still talk about county seats, we do not talk about county capitals.

Federalism, then, is quite different from decentralization. It is not at all on the same continuum. This difference can be demonstrated most easily when we contrast federal polities with other forms of political organization. In all of the history of study, speculation, and empirical research about political systems, political philosophers and political scientists have come up with essentially three models of polity: the hierarchical model, the organic model, and the federal model. From Plato and Aristotle or the *Bible* before them, right down to the latest work that is published in the journals of political science, implicitly or explicitly, we find those three models of political organization and development. In the very first essay in *The Federalist*, Alexander Hamilton presents the Constitutional ratification issue by stating that it is given to the American people to determine whether they shall have a government established by "force," or "accident," or "reflection and choice."

Now "force" is a polemical way of identifying a hierarchical system since hierarchical systems are essentially established by force. Political philosophers and scientists alike see hierarchical systems as having been established first by conquest after which the conqueror imposes a power pyramid on a community or a body politic. "Accident" refers to polities that have developed organically; in other words, whatever happened to happen, happened and the people get the system that results. Finally, there are those political systems which have been established by the deliberate acts— "reflection and choice"—of those who are to be the citizens of the polity, who come together and by some act of covenanting or compacting establish a body politic. This is the highest form of political constitution according to *The Federalist*. There are various combinations and permutations and variations of the three models but there are only three models.

The Hierarchical Model

The hierarchical model has its origins in ancient Egypt. It is no accident that the pharoahs built pyramids to mark and commemorate their respective persons because the Egyptian system was a power pyramid. The pharoah was on top, indeed he was a god or a demi–god. He governed through a hierarchy of control and the whole pyramid rested on the Egyptian people. That is the way of power pyramids.

Whenever we talk about the American system as a system of levels of government, we have implicitly adopted the power pyramid model. Nobody talked that way about the United States in the nineteenth century. That terminology was not introduced until well into the twentieth century, after students of politics began to absorb ideas derived from traditional management and organization theory with its hierarchical emphasis on chains of command. Management as we know it, modern management, is derived from the military models developed by the French and the Prussians, which were hierarchical. Woodrow Wilson, the father of the study of public administration in the United States, wrote his great essay on *The Study of Public Administration* based on French and particularly German models. So, too, did his colleagues in the late nineteenth century—for good reason, because if you want a managerial system, there is something to be said on behalf of that kind of structure, at least up to a point. But those ideas were then transposed from good management sense to a kind of managerialism which saw the whole world as properly organized in that way, and we began to talk about the United States as having levels of government: the federal government on the top, the states as the middle level, the local governments as the lower level (Figure 1). Implicitly, there were the people back underneath the pyramid again, just as in the days of ancient Egypt.

Today, this model has given us a terminology which just rolls off our tongues; we do not even think about it. Yet it is a model that challenges the very fundaments of federal democracy. If you look in a nineteenth century textbook of American government at a chart of how the American system is organized, what you usually find is something like this: the people are on top, the Constitution is the mediating force between the people and their institutions, and the federal and state governments are presented as equals. Look at a government textbook today and you see instead that power pyramid: the federal government on the top, the states in the middle, local governments underneath. The charts never mention the people or the Constitution. The people are there, all

FIGURE 1

The Hierarchical Model

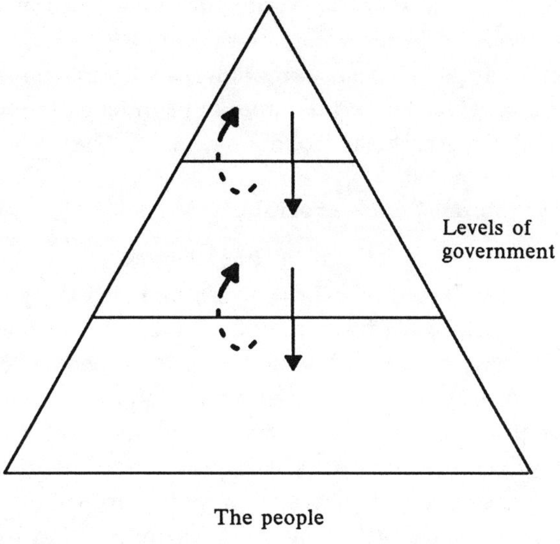

right—but in that hierarchical structure, the Constitution is hardly there at all.

Today we know what the consequences of that reconceptualization were. Fifteen years ago, we had to contend with the imperial presidency. That was only natural. If there is a governmental pyramid, there has to be an apex. If there is to be somebody at the apex of an American pyramid, it is going to be the President; he became the center of attention, the focus of all the media. And so Americans began to believe that not only was the federal government superior to the states, but the President was superior to Congress. It would require another paper to describe how that came about. However, presidents began to believe their press releases. So John F. Kennedy and Lyndon Johnson got the United States into the Vietnam War by presidential manipulation and Richard Nixon gave Americans Watergate by exercising what he called "executive privilege." These were only two of the most visible and painful consequences of the imperial presidency following the patterns of the hierarchical model.

The Organic or Center–Periphery Model

The organic model can be traced back to ancient Mesopotamia. It was reflected in their religion, in which the gods were conceived as members of a common council, an elite governing the universe. Each god had his or her favorite people, whose task it was to provide support for their special god or goddess. The gods were at the center of the universe and the people around their periphery. This system was a little more open than that of ancient Egypt, in the sense that it was an oligarchy instead of an autocracy; there was no single person or god at the apex—they were all sitting around the same table, as it were. The senior god, known as Zeus in Greek or Jupiter in Roman mythology, presided at the head of the table, but he did not sit on top of a pyramid.

This center–periphery model of classic Western polytheism describes the way in which certain political systems have developed, just as the hierarchical model does for others. France, a nice democratic republic, is a good example of the hierarchical model. It is a state that was established by conquest as the county of Paris expanded its domains and, accordingly, ruled hierarchically from Paris, the capital. Britain, particularly England, is a good example of the organic model. It developed by expanding its territory, creating a center with the interlocking of petty rulers, giving each a share in the larger whole. Then, over time, as it developed organically, it expanded access to and participation in that center. The introduction of representative government in both France and Britain institutionalized what became, in time, the democratic republican dimensions of both polities, but France still remained a pyramid and Britain a center with a periphery. In Britain, if you are not in London, you are nowhere and in France, if you are not in Paris, you are nowhere.

The organic model is constructed so that the center makes the crucial political decisions. In Britain, Parliament (which technically includes King, Lords, and Commons) is that center. You may have heard Walter Bagehot's classic description of the British Parliament: that if Parliament chose to legislate a man into a woman or a woman into a man, it would have the sovereign power to do so. (This was said before individuals could do that surgically.) Parliament is representative of the estates and territories of Britain. Today, the peripheries are represented democratically in the center, but it is still the center that decides. We have a current example of this before us. Prime Minister Margaret Thatcher has decided to reduce the power of the local government in Britain. If she can carry a majority in Parliament, she can do so; there are no constitutional barriers to that, regardless of the opposition of the local authorities.

FIGURE 2

The Center–Periphery Model

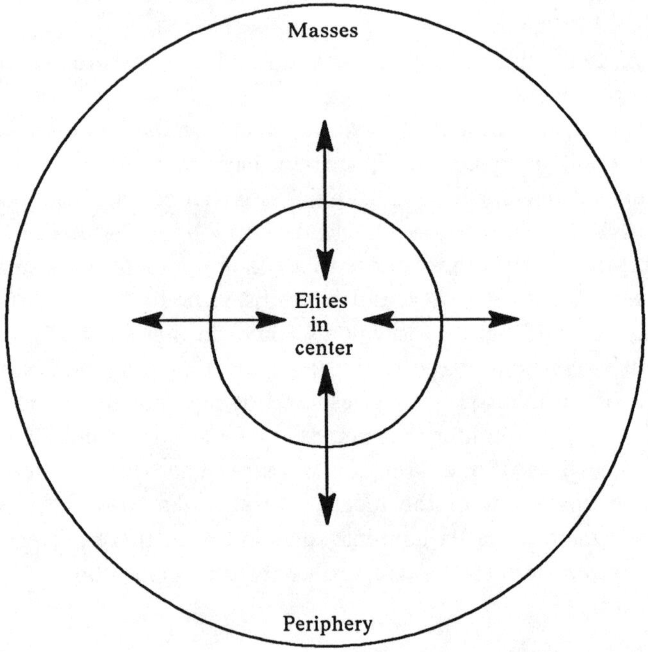

The Federal Model

How would we describe the federal model, if it is neither a power pyramid nor a center with a periphery? I would suggest that the federal model is best described as a matrix. Think of it as a big square or rectangle, in which the federal, or general, government is the framing institution enclosing its basic constituent units, which may be further divided into local governments. What we have is a congeries of arenas, boxes inside boxes, of different sizes, smaller and larger.

What does this suggest? In a power pyramid, inevitably, the higher one is the more important. In a center–periphery model, the more central one is, the more important. In contrast, smaller and larger in the federal model does not mean or cannot dictate the degree of importance. The federal matrix suggests that for certain purposes, smaller arenas are more important and for others, larger arenas are, but that smaller or larger in itself does not *a priori* determine or define importance. Hence it is in the federal matrix that it is possible to develop the best combination of self–rule and shared rule, of having one's cake and eating it too, of wanting to go and wanting to stay. It offers the best possibility for the synthesis of George Mason's argument that without community there is no liberty, and James Madison's argument that without an extended republic where there can be so many competing interests that polarization of the two classes can be prevented, liberty cannot survive.

In a federal matrix, the largest arena is designed to undertake those tasks and protect those rights that have to be undertaken or protected collectively to achieve and preserve the purposes of the polity, while smaller arenas can function to provide appropriate scale or appropriate community. That, again, is the essence of any federal arrangement and is at the heart of federal theory.

The matrix then, is both a matrix of power and a matrix of arenas. Just as the hierarchical model derived in our time from theories of administration and management which emphasized the

FIGURE 3

The Federal Model

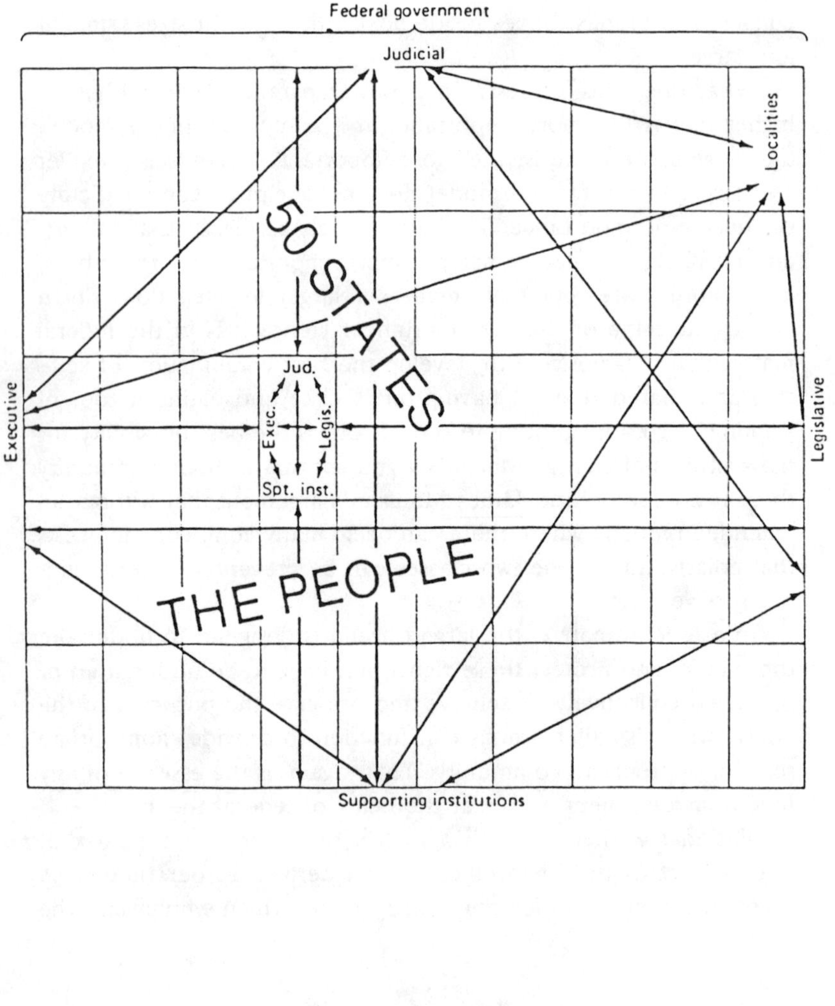

importance of the chain of command, and the center–periphery model derived from theories of elite–and–mass, which emphasized the necessity to concentrate power in certain elites in order to govern effectively and to deal with the masses, the federal model also has a relationship to the cybernetic theory of human organization. Cybernetic theory states that the best way to organize things is through multiple channels, intelligent redundancy, fail safe mechanisms, and multiple cells linked together so that not every cell has to function perfectly in order for the system to work. Martin Landau, one of the leading professors of public administration of our time, has suggested that the founding fathers two hundred years ago anticipated cybernetic theory and that the federal model is, indeed, the governmental equivalent of a cybernetic model.

Take a look at the matrix again. Think of it as a power grid in which political power, governmental power, courses through like electricity. In some cases, we load certain elements in the grid with greater power and in others, we load other elements in the grid, perhaps with lesser power. In the United States, foreign affairs and defense are loaded on that element which frames the whole, the federal government. The heavy loadings for education are placed on the local arenas, while those for highway construction are placed on the state arenas. These loadings can be shifted in a variety of ways, depending on what is more likely to achieve the various goals which the publics in a particular system set for themselves. A look at the high level career patterns and salaries reflect this distribution. The power pinnacle in highway administration is to become the head of the state highway department of one of the great states of the American union. The most important positions in elementary and secondary educational administration are those of the superintendents of the major school systems—not necessarily the big city school systems either; to be superintendent of an important suburban school system may be one of the most important positions in the profession at a given time.

This matrix is federal because it is established by the coming together of individuals or individual polities as equals to establish the political order. From the beginning, the federal model involves the active consent of equals. The very term federal comes from the Latin *foedus*, which means covenant. Classically, a covenant involves both separating and uniting. Indeed, in the semitic languages of the ancient Near East, where the idea of covenanting first emerged, making a covenant is referred to as "cutting a covenant." In the *Bible*, ancient covenanting is described as literally involving a ritual act in which the parties who were binding themselves took an animal, sacrificed it by cutting it in half, passed between the two halves of the animal, and then bound the pieces of the animal together. In other words, the cutting is to assure that both parties recognize their separate integrities as partners to the covenant and the binding is to demonstrate that they are partners and are truly linked. Federalism involves covenanting and the partnership that flows from it. It is a model in which people, institutions, or polities covenant or compact together to form a larger whole in which their own equality and their respective integrities are preserved, along with the establishment of the new framing entity. Federalism, in the last analysis, involves a linkage between this covenant and the partnership it creates.

Americans know this from their historical experience, even if only subconsciously. If Americans should ever, heaven forfend, have to adopt a formal salutation as the Communist regimes have adopted "comrade," I have no doubt in my mind that they would choose the term used by the archetypical American folk hero, the cowboy: "pardner" or "pard." The interesting thing is that in those federal systems serving civil societies with truly federal political cultures, similar terms are to be found. In Australia, the equivalent is "mate." These terms describe federal human relationships and ties.

Conclusion

Both George Mason and James Madison accepted this fundamental theory, even as they diverged in recommending how it should be applied. Mason's critique, as I have suggested, was that the only system that would work to preserve the values of federalism would be small republic federalism or confederation. Only in that way, where there could be face to face community or something close to it, could the civil and political rights of citizens be preserved. Otherwise, there would be federal encroachment on local liberties, willy-nilly. If the largest arena were too large, it would lose touch. If it lost touch, it would be transformed, sooner or later, into a power pyramid; that has been the history and the fate of so much of the human race.

Madison, as I suggested, argued differently. Both were right. As we look at the two hundred years of experience with federalism in the United States, we can see not only how right Mason has been in so many ways but also how we need to reform the system to regain what we have lost as a result of the overemphasis on the federal government's role. It is the task of those of us who have been born into the way of James Madison and who genuinely believe that on balance, what Madison proposed was necessary and right, to be aware of George Mason's critique of the United States Constitution. We must try to include in the substance of the federal system those elements which Mason wanted us to consider as much as the elements that Madison wanted us to consider.

Notes

1. It is important to note that the term "republican" did not come into general use in a positive sense until the winter of 1775–76 as the colonies moved toward independence through their new union, "the United States in Congress assembled." See Donald S. Lutz, *Popular Consent and Popular Control* (Baton Rouge: University of Louisiana Press, 1980), 1–22.

2. For an analysis of the Declaration, see my "The Declaration of Independence: The Founding Covenant of the American People," a working paper of the Workshop on Covenant and Politics of the Center for the Study of Federalism, Temple University (Philadelphia, 1981).

3

Federalism: The Contemporary Challenge

ROBERT B. HAWKINS, JR.
Chairman,
Advisory Commission on Intergovernmental Relations

FEDERALISM IS A UNIQUE AMERICAN INVENTION. IT deals with the division of powers and responsibilities—and sometimes the overlap of these—between the national and state governments. However, the broad concept of federalism provides neither clear nor precise answers about the best way to divide the functions of government among the levels or how to fashion the most productive intergovernmental relationships where the functions overlap. The answers shift with the ebb and flow of history.

In recent decades, the intertwining of functional responsibilities among the levels of government in the United States has become so complex that the focus on intergovernmental relations (and on the administrative processes that support them) overshadowed the basic issues of federalism. The contemporary challenge, then, is to redirect our attention to the fundamental division of powers between the national and state levels. As America's experiment in federalism has been copied by other nations, especially in the last four decades, we have gained foreign perspectives that might help to clarify our thinking on this issue.

This paper reviews the concept of federalism, examines the history of federalism in the United States, and explores the contemporary need to focus anew on the basic principles of federalism.

The Concept of Federalism

The American colonies were not strong enough to stand alone against the oppressive power of England, so they banded together in revolution and emerged as a confederation of states that preserved state sovereignty and relied upon the states themselves to carry out national purposes. By 1787, it had become obvious that the Confederation was not adequate to the tasks of national defense, foreign relations, and promotion of a strong national economy. A Constitutional Convention was convened to replace the Articles of Confederation with a plan for a stronger national government. That convention launched our nation on the sea of federalism.

The Constitution and Dual Federalism

The sea of federalism was totally uncharted when the Constitutional Convention convened.[1] The nationalists at the Convention rallied around the Virginia Plan presented by Edmund Randolph. This plan provided for a bicameral congress, based on direct election of the lower house and that house's selection of an upper house. This congress would have had a very broad but general grant of powers including the power to override the states. Setting aside the question of the composition of congress, the Convention rather quickly adopted the principle that an independent national government was to be established with legislative, executive, and judicial components. However, at this point, those delegates committed to continuing state sovereignty dug in their heels and forced a series of compromises that resulted in a dual system of government with a limited set of enumerated powers for the national level, equal representation of the states in the upper house of Congress, state control over the process of naming presidential electors (equal in number to their representation in Congress), and establishing the judiciary rather than the Congress as the arbitrator of disputes between the national and state governments. Through these compromises, the "balance of powers" concept that had been applied within the national government—with acceptance of legislative, executive, judicial components—was applied again as between the national government and the states. A division of functional powers, and representation, and adjudication of disputes among the levels was built into the Constitution to provide a measure of "sovereignty" at *both* levels of government. This became known as the concept of "dual federalism," and it was afforded considerable deference, if not always strict practical adherence, for the next 140 years.

Democracy, Pluralism, and Freedom

The size of government, and its closeness to the people, are points that have been raised in arguments both for and against establishing large national governments.[2] The Antifederalists at the Constitutional Convention argued against a sovereign national component in the Constitution on the basis that the smaller state governments would be more responsive to their citizens and more controllable. Therefore, they argued, sovereignty should remain at the level closest to the people. However, in supporting a constitutional provision for a sovereign national government, Madison argued in *The Federalist*, No. 10 that smaller governments would more likely be controlled by a strong majority, based on a more homogeneous population, and would more likely oppress its minorities. Thus, he argued for a strong national government encompassing multiple minorities and protecting their rights as well as the rights of individuals. The truth in each of these diametrically opposed arguments makes a strong theoretical case for the type of *dual* federalism established by the Constitution—and so does such current research as we have on this issue. These mixed research results indicate that: (1) national elections attract the greatest participation; (2) most people surveyed believe that local governments are more understandable and controllable than are distant units; and (3) surveyed citizens place greater confidence in state and local governments than in the national government. Thus, there is some empirical, as well as theoretical, justification for the dual nature of our federal system.

The Division of Powers

The theory of federalism emerging from the Constitution establishes the principle that the powers of government should be divided between the levels, and enumerates several that are preeminently national. However, the Constitution goes on to authorize very general powers of national taxing and spending for the general welfare, while stating (in the Tenth Amendment) that all other powers are reserved to the states or to the people.

Thus, beyond the enumerated national powers, our Constitution leaves us with very little guidance about the relative roles of state and nation. This constitutional ambiguity led Woodrow Wilson to observe, in 1908, that "the relationship of the states to the federal government is the cardinal question of our Constitutional system," and he observed that this question cannot be permanently resolved because "every successive stage of our political and economic development gives it a new aspect, makes it a new question." This implies that whatever Congress and the courts agree upon from one decade to the next is our definition of federalism for that time.

Nevertheless, scholars continue to wrestle with this issue in an attempt to find a more principled basis for allocating the functions of government among the levels. The Advisory Commission on Intergovernmental Relations (ACIR) catalogued the common criteria being used a decade ago, and found them to fall within four general categories: political accountability, equity (or fairness), administrative effectiveness, and economic efficiency.[3] Political accountability implies both access to the elected and appointed officials making significant public choices, and the ability to influence them. It encompasses the merits and demerits of both the electoral process and a whole variety of citizen participation mechanisms at each level of government. The equity concept involves fairness in providing and paying for services for the betterment of both the citizens of the given jurisdiction and those of neighboring jurisdictions when spillover effects occur. Program needs and ability to pay are important components of this concept. Administrative effectiveness has elements such as geographic adequacy, legal adequacy, management capability, and intergovernmental flexibility. The economic efficiency concept includes elements such as economies of scale, public sector competition, and the pricing of public services at each level of government.

These criteria apply differently to different functions of government and even to the various activities within the major functions. In addition, various criteria often tend to conflict with one another. For example, spillover effects (like pollution originating in one jurisdiction fouling the air or water in another) might be solved most easily by enlarging the jurisdiction to encompass the spillover, but the larger government might be less politically accountable and might reduce public service competition. Thus, technical analysis of these criteria may provide useful information for public debate, but political judgment is required to weigh the values of one criterion against those of the others.

In recent years, there has been a major increase in research on criteria for making rational choices on economic grounds, especially concerning the pricing of public services, competitive contracting for services to keep prices down and improve service quality, and the use of smaller units of government to provide a greater choice of service and tax levels to the public.

Foreign Perspectives

A recent ACIR study[4] examined the status of federalism in Australia, Canada, the United States, and West Germany to see how they compare in: (1) matching financial resources to functional responsibilities at each level of government; (2) setting minimum national standards for certain basic services; (3) equalizing the tax efforts required by the various subnational governments to meet their functional responsibilities; and (4) coordinating the fiscal systems of the levels of government. The study found that each country approached these tasks differently. West Germany had the most formal system. It is based upon detailed provisions in its Basic Law (constitution) spelling out in substantial detail the division of functions and the sharing of tax sources among the levels of government. The Basic Law also provides for a Laender (state)-controlled house in the national legislature for the purpose of reviewing legislation affecting the Laenders and vetoing any legislation found objectionable. Any law thus vetoed by a two-thirds majority of this house, the Bundesrat, can be re-enacted only by a two-thirds majority vote of the popularly elected Bundestag.

Australia and Canada also have systematic mechanisms for dealing with intergovernmental issues, but they are based more heavily upon executive negotiations. In Australia, the annual Premiers' Conference sets the basic tone for federal-state relations each year, while the Grants Commission and the Loan Council, respectively, allocate the national grants among the states in a strongly equalizing fashion and apportion annual governmental borrowing authority (with some exceptions like defense) among the subnational units. Canada also begins with an annual meeting of the first ministers (the Prime Minister and the ten Provincial Ministers), and then follows up with a large number of meetings of deputy ministers and senior departmental officers in which negotiations are used to resolve a wide array of intergovernmental issues. Canada also has a formal program of national equalizing payments to those provinces with tax yields below a specified standard.

The United States has the least formal and least systematic process for approaching these intergovernmental issues. The main mechanism is a complex system of several hundred federal grants. Each grant program is enacted separately, administered relatively independently within the executive branch, and adjudicated from time-to-time by the federal courts. The General Revenue Sharing program of the past decade-and-a-half has been the only substantial effort to provide some measure of equalization among the subnational units of government. Although there is a special analysis in the President's annual budget concerning federal aid to state and local governments, that topic has not received systematic attention in the congressional budget process. ACIR is the only official national body concerned with intergovernmental relations, and its role is strictly advisory. Thus, issues of federalism and intergovernmental relations in the United States are addressed primarily through political lobbying by the states and local governments in the national legislative process, and on a case–by–case basis in the courts.

On a comparative basis, then, federalism and intergovernmental relations issues are addressed in the United States on a less orderly basis and with less commitment to fiscal equalization among the levels of government than in the other nations studied. Nevertheless, American local governments play a more vital role than in the other nations, and in particular, exert much more influence at the national level, although by informal political means. By the same token, the American states have weaker Constitutional status than their counterparts in West Germany, Australia, and Canada. Overall, the U.S. federal system comes closer to having three equal tiers of government than these other nations. And the relationships among these three tiers are hammered out year–by–year in the rough and tumble process of political give and take.

The History of U.S. Federalism: Judicial, Fiscal, Regulatory and Programmatic Dimensions

As mentioned at the outset, federalism in the United States is constantly changing. It has gone through a number of stages since the Constitution was ratified. Four eras stand out. The first, known as Dual Federalism, maintained a separation between state and national functions, by–and–large, for the nation's first 140 years under the Constitution. Then, beginning with the Great Depression, the national government began to expand its domestic functions in cooperation with the states and localities. This second era, called Cooperative Federalism, lasted until the mid–1960s when a tremendous explosion of federal grant programs and federal regulations began to dominate many state and local functions, often setting off controversial and stressful relationships rather than cooperative ones. This third era, called Overloaded Federalism, lasted until 1981 when President Reagan introduced his New Federalism as a means of reversing federal dominance. Each of these eras deserves a brief examination.

Dual Federalism (1789–1929)[5]

This 140–year era of Dual Federalism was split almost exactly in half by the Civil War. Until that war, the old arguments of the Constitutional Convention about national supremacy vs. state sovereignty continued to build in political circles. The Bill of Rights and the Eleventh Amendment, both added shortly after the Constitution itself was ratified, sought to affirm that national powers were limited and state powers were protected. The Supreme Court adjudicated a few cases of conflict between the federal and state levels before the Civil War, favoring one side sometimes, and then the other. But, functionally, the federal bureaucracy stuck to the limited functions enumerated in the Constitution and remained quite small. Most domestic functions of government remained in the hands of the states and their localities, with very little regular or required interchange with the national government. Revenue sources also were separate, with the federal government relying primarily on customs fees and revenues from the sale of western lands, while the states relied largely on excise taxes, and the local governments stuck to the property tax. Intergovernmental aid was rare and not regularized.

The Civil War stopped the contention between the arguments for national supremacy and those for state sovereignty and led to a Supreme Court decision in the 1869 case of *Texas v. White* that clearly stated the Dual Federalism concept: "The Constitution, in all its provisions, looks to an indestructible Union composed of indestructible States." As a result of the war, three constitutional amendments, a cluster of civil rights acts, and a highly intrusive national law concerning reconstruction in the southern states were enacted, and the Supreme Court stepped up its review of federalism cases. Functionally, the federal government gradually became more active in regulating the increasingly nationwide economy, encouraging economic development through public works, conserving natural resources, and contributing in limited ways to social welfare and higher education. However, the Supreme Court limited the impact of the post–Civil War amendments and laws, leaving civil and voting rights matters largely to the states until the 1950s and 1960s. Most governmental services continued to be provided at the local level.

By 1927, near the end of the Dual Federalism era, state and local tax collections still accounted for nearly twice as much as those of the federal government, and the personnel at the state and local levels were four times the number at the national level. Thus, the state and local governments remained the senior partners for most domestic programs. Local governments carried out nearly one–half of all public services, and had no regular contact with the federal government.

Yet, the seeds of the coming Cooperative Federalism era had been planted in two respects. First, federal revenues had switched heavily to the income tax source, as had some states; revenue overlapping had begun. Second, intergovernmental aid had begun to become a significant factor. By 1929, state aid to local governments equaled nearly one–third of state collected revenues, and the federal government had 15 programs of grants to the states equaling about 4% of its revenue.

Cooperative Federalism (1930–1963)

The era of the Great Depression and recovery from World War War II brought dramatic changes in the role of the federal government. In its efforts to bring about recovery from the depression and readjustment from a wartime to a peacetime economy, numerous national programs of a domestic nature were established where none had existed previously. For the first time, the national government took responsibility for the health of the nation's economy; it much more actively regulated businesses; it intervened in labor–management relations; and it began stimulating many activities in regional development, urban affairs, transportation, and the health and welfare fields.

The Supreme Court, at first, was reluctant to condone these new moves, but it finally broadened its interpretation of the Interstate Commerce Clause and the constitutional provisions for spending on the general welfare by the late 1930s to remove virtually all obstacles to the expansion of national programs.

Massive expansion of the federal income tax, plus enactment and judicial ratification of the social security tax, also brought the federal government into the dominant position in governmental finance during this period. State taxes also diversified and increased during this era, while local revenues declined in proportion, continuing to rely largely upon the property tax source. Although there was some overlap between federal and state tax sources, the revenue system remained relatively compartmentalized, with 96% of income taxes going to the federal treasury, 94% of property taxes staying at the local level, and consumption taxes of various sorts being tapped fairly exclusively by either the states or the federal government.

The relative decline in local revenue strength led to major increases in programs of both federal and state aid. This movement gave rise to regularized intergovernmental relationships and brought the federal government, as well as the states, into direct and regular contact with many local governments. Throughout most of this era, state aid to local governments ran significantly ahead of federal aid to the states and localities, and the bulk of federal aid went to the states.

Most of the federal aid was for programs eagerly sought by the state and local governments; it was administered cooperatively; and it was condoned by the courts as collaboration rather than coercion. Although federal aid was conditioned upon certain requirements for building up state and local planning and administrative capabilities, and for stimulating greater programmatic activity in certain functions, the federal programs seldom dominated the activity and the grant conditions, in comparison with those in later years, were minimal.

Overloaded Federalism (1964–1980)

By the mid–1960s, the federal government was firmly established in the intergovernmental aid field, and set to massively increase the number of programs of intergovernmental aid and to embark upon major new forms of regulation affecting the states and their localities.[6] Over the next 15 years, the federal government moved toward dominance in many domestic activities of government previously assumed to be primarily in the realm of subnational units.

As the federal government moved toward this wider scope of activities, its programs began to empower the poor against the local government establishment, to protect victims of past discrimination, and to foster a number of additional national goals. Moreover, special grants for each purpose multiplied, taking the number of grants during this era from 51 to more than 500 and raising the average proportion of federal aid in state and local budgets from about 15% to nearly 24%.[7] This new degree of dependence on federal aid grew even higher in many needy central cities.

As the number and financial magnitude of federal grants multiplied, so did the federal mandates attached to them. Almost every grant became a vehicle for meeting national environmental, civil rights, handicapped access, relocation, historical preservation, citizen participation, and planning standards. In addition, the federal government mandated detailed standards for budgeting, reporting, auditing, property acquisition and control, and other administrative standards.[8] Other federal regulations set rules for state and local governments in drawing electoral boundaries, governing election campaign financing, protecting occupational safety and health, paying construction wages, and negotiating labor contracts.[9]

These often confrontational national policies generated massive amounts of new litigation, and most of the cases upheld federal dominance in these matters. The federal courts not only acceded to the judgment of Congress in most cases, but even went beyond the vagueness of laws to supply concrete operational interpretations and direct administrative remedies in such matters as school busing and overcrowding in prisons and other public institutions.

The added costs and red-tape of these intrusive federal mandates began turning many state and local beneficiaries of federal programs into critics during the 1970s. Federal-aid simplification efforts cropped up here and there, but with only marginal results. The five block grants enacted during this time, to help simplify administration and enhance flexibility, suffered recategorization pressures. State and local governments took few initiatives without first inquiring about what the relevant federal programs would require. Federal intrusion was pervasive and deep.

New Federalism (1981–Present)

With the inauguration of President Reagan, the administration's philosophy of federalism took a clear turn toward devolution. The President's deeply held belief that too many functions of government had ascended to the national level was very evident in his 1981 budget revisions for fiscal year 1982 called "America's New Beginning: A Program for Economic Recovery," and in his 1982 and 1983 federalism initiatives.

Federal fiscal problems have both spurred and tainted the moves toward a new federalism. The hard-fought budget battles of 1981 resulted, late in the year, in the adoption of a FY 1982 budget that made one of the most far-reaching revisions to the federal–aid system ever adopted in one package. This budget merged over 70 grant programs into a number of new and revised block grants, raising the total number of such flexible aid programs from 5 to 11, and substantially reducing federal program guidance and paperwork requirements in them. In addition, approximately 60 additional grant programs were terminated. The terminated programs included most planning assistance to local, state, and regional units, and were accompanied by substantial reductions in funds in certain other programs like economic development. In addition, the federal government withdrew its participation from multistate economic development and water resources planning commissions, and abolished federal regional councils that had been organized under President Nixon to coordinate federal aid to state and local governments. The rationale for abolishing these federal regional councils was that most federal aid would shift to the states and be in the form of block grants requiring little federal administrative tracking.

Thus, in one short year, the total number of grant programs dropped from 540 to 405, and federal–aid dollars were reduced by 6.6 billion. In the minds of many state and local officials this action equated New Federalism with budget cutting, and spurred resistance to further federalism initiatives. However, even with this resistance, and with some nominal increases in federal–aid dollars for fiscal years 1983 and 1984, the buying power of federal aid to state and local governments dropped 15% over the 1980–1984 period.

President's Reagan's 1982 and 1983 federalism initiatives continued the debate over returning governmental functions to the states and localities. The 1982 initiative proposed a national take–over of the Medicaid program in exchange for state take–over of food stamps and basic welfare responsibilities, such as Aid to Families with Dependent Children. It also proposed combining 40 more federal grant programs into four broad block grants. This proposal received serious consideration from the nation's governors during a nearly year–long negotiation process, but in the end it bore no fruit. When the President renewed his federalism initiative in 1983, the federal–state swap was omitted, the number of federal–aid programs to be blocked was reduced slightly, and the nature of the four mega–blocks was changed. The 1982 proposal had been for four functional block grants in the fields of education, community development, transportation, and social services. The four mega–blocks for 1983 would have included: (1) a massive state block grant encompassing 22 education, health, social services, and community development programs; (2) a federal–local block grant combining general revenue sharing and the entitlement portion of the community development block grant; (3) a limited transportation block grant; and (4) a rural housing block grant. In both the 1982 and 1983 federalism initiatives, the new block grants were designed as transitional steps in turning these functions of government, and specified federal revenue resources, back to the state and local governments. Although submitted to the Congress with implementing legislation, no hearings were held and no other action was taken on the 1983 federalism initiative.

The Reagan administration also pursued a vigorous Regulatory Relief Program during its first term, about 25% of which was designed to reduce burdens on state and local governments. By August 1982, the Presidential Task Force on Regulatory Relief chaired by the Vice–President estimated that its efforts would save state and local governments about $2 billion per year.[10]

On the judicial front, little has happened to reverse federal intrusions into state and local affairs. To the contrary, the courts have increased federal intrusiveness in at least two ways. In Decision No. 821913 handed down on February 19, 1985, the Supreme Court not only reversed its 1977 decision in the case of *National League of Cities v. Usery* and applied federal labor standards to all state and local employees, but also took itself out of future "commerce power" disputes between the states and the national government.

A second series of cases opened local governments to liability under the Sherman Antitrust Act, including triple monetary damages, for a variety of monopolistic or regulatory activities, unless localities are given immunity by their state.[11] Under these decisions, many normal local activities like cable television franchising, zoning, the issuance of permits for utility hookups, and franchising taxi cabs, all were thrown into legal doubt. At the end of its 1984 session, Congress enacted an exemption to the Sherman Antitrust Act removing the threat of monetary damages against local governments and individual local officials, but let stand the prohibition against local activities that could be construed as restraining competition.

Since the beginning of Cooperative Federalism in the 1930s, federal aid heavily stimulated the modernization of state and local governments and nudged them into many new activities. Along with the efforts of the state and local units themselves, this stimulation brought the capabilities of state and local governments to new heights by the beginning of the New Federalism era. ACIR has tracked these transformations[12] and found the states to be organized far more effectively in both their executive and legislative branches than they were just two decades ago, local governments having much greater discretionary authority (including substantial diversification of revenue sources), and county governments, in particular, being much better organized and more capable of providing needed services in urban areas. This record of capacity-building at the state and local levels, and the relative fiscal health of these levels when compared to the huge federal deficits being faced in the mid-1980s, placed these subnational units in a favorable position to take on a greater share of the responsibility for governing our nation.

The Contemporary Issue: Return to a More Equal Balance of Powers

The foregoing history of our nation's nearly 200 years under the Constitution brings us to the conclusion that the national government is the senior partner in most respects; it has far outstripped the states and their localities in both power and influence. Madison argued very effectively in *The Federalist*, Nos. 45 and 46, that this would not happen. Some of the states, of course, feared this result from the outset, but Madison countered that:

1. The federal government would depend on state representation in electing the President through the electoral college under the supervision of the state legislatures, and by having the state legislatures appoint members of the United States Senate.
2. The states would command the weight of personal influence in governmental affairs because of superior numbers of elected officials, bureaucrats, militia, tax collectors, and other functionaries.
3. Federal powers would be few, well defined, and limited largely to those exercised in time of war or danger, while state powers would be numerous, indefinite, and predominant during normal times of peace and security.
4. The same citizens that support both levels of government would be much more inclined to support the more familiar and directly relevant services produced by the states, and would also be more supportive of the state and local governments that provide the larger number of job benefits and well known officials.
5. The members of Congress would have little reason or inclination to invade the state's prerogatives, but if they do, the states would have ample incentive and means to resist ambitious federal encroachments, including access to the state militia and support from their citizens who would retain the right to bear arms.

Although these arguments seemed eminently sensible and carried the day during the ratification of the Constitution, they are no longer persuasive:

1. Members of the United States Senate no longer are appointed by the state legislatures, and the states' connections to Congress have weakened very considerably.

2. Although the numbers of state and local officials, and the size of their bureaucracies, remain much larger than their federal counterparts, this makes little difference now that pervasive federal programs and federal court orders have so frequently co-opted them into national service.
3. Federal powers now are anything but limited, and the commerce power, that was specifically cited by Madison as causing little apprehension among the states, now is one of the most common justifications for the expansion of federal power.
4. The citizenry now seems to approve of a greatly expanded federal role — which Madison agreed would be legitimate, although he thought highly unlikely — largely because the state and local governments did not or could not achieve desired results on their own.
5. Although the pork barrel and other parochial issues still roam the halls of Congress, national issues predominate in a way never dreamed of by Madison. In fact, every issue seems to become a national issue, spurred on by the national media. The state militia and citizens bearing arms are of little help to the states in opposing federal court orders and resisting dominant federal fiscal resources. Civil protests sometimes are effective in drawing attention to the need for redress on national issues, but the state resistance envisioned by Madison is a thing of the past.

The Goal

With these collapsing constraints on federal power, and the subordination of state and local governments in program–after–program, our system has become unbalanced; national power has become too great. Our goal, then, must be to reestablish a greater separation of governmental functions among the levels of government and to return greater authority and influence to the states and to their political subdivisions. Only then will the benefits of our federal system of government be realized once again, benefits like: (1) limited governments with countervailing forces among the levels, keeping each in check; (2) greater opportunities for the expression of full democratic choice at each level of government, and especially at those levels closest to the people; and (3) retention of the states as laboratories of democracy where new ideas can be tried and new variations tested without putting the whole nation at risk.

The Advisory Commission on Intergovernmental Relations, in fact, has called for such a return to the basic principles of Constitutional Federalism.

> The Commission recommends a reassessment of legal doctrines delimiting the boundaries of national Constitutional authority vis-a-vis the reserved powers of the states so that those reserved powers again become meaningful and viable. To help restore a sense of balance between the levels of government, the Commission urges reconsideration by the national legislative, executive and judicial branches of current interpretations of the commerce and spending powers....[13]
>
> The Commission recommends that Congress and the Administration carefully consider the appropriate allocation of responsibilities among the different levels of government when establishing new... programs or when evaluating existing ones. As a general principle, the Commission strongly recommends that the federal government strive to confine its regulation of state and local governments and their legitimate activities to the minimum level consistent with compelling national interest. Enactment of federal intergovernmental regulation may be warranted under the following circumstances:
>
> 1) to protect basic political and civil rights guaranteed to all American citizens under the Constitution;
>
> 2) to ensure national defense and the proper conduct of foreign affairs;
>
> 3) to establish certain uniform and minimum standards in areas affecting the flow of interstate commerce;
>
> 4) to prevent state and local actions which substantially and adversely affect another state or its citizens; or
>
> 5) to assure essential fiscal and programmatic integrity in the use of federal grants and contracts into which state and local governments freely enter.

> The Commission emphasizes, however, that these criteria do not justify every federal...action that has tenuous relationship to one or more of these principles. Rather, federal intergovernmental regulation is warranted only when a clear and convincing case has demonstrated both the necessity of such intervention and a marked inability of state and local governments to address the...problem involved. In making this determination, the Commission strongly believes that the criteria above must be weighed against the federal government's commensurate responsibility to maintain the viability of the federal system and to respect the institutional integrity of states and their localities.
>
> If, according to this test, the federal government's involvement in a...program is appropriate, the Commission further recommends that the federal government choose the least intrusive means...consistent with the national interest, allowing state and local governments the maximum degree of flexibility permissible.[14]

Potential Means of Rebalancing Federalism

If we, as a nation, are serious about rebalancing federalism and returning greater authority to the states to restore the balance of powers and the great opportunities for diversity and innovation promised by the Constitution, and if we feel as strongly committed to this goal as to some of the other provisions of the Constitution—like the guarantees of personal freedom and voting rights—we must consider practical and concrete means of moving in that direction. I offer, here, eight such suggestions:

1. Reinforce national fiscal constraints.
2. Strengthen the state-initiated constitutional amendment process.
3. Introduce national referenda and initiatives.
4. Reconstitute the United States Senate with members appointed by the state legislatures.
5. Give the state and local political parties campaign finance rights equal to the national political parties.
6. Use the federal grant system to play a much stronger role in fiscal equalization among the states.
7. Enable the states and localities to respond more adequately to the needs of their citizens.
8. Reinvigorate judicial federalism.

Let us examine each of these proposals briefly.

National Fiscal Constraints: One of the principal reasons for national fiscal dominance was adoption of the income tax during wartime and the retention and expansion of that revenue source since World War I. That tax is the most productive one in the nation, and it has grown rapidly with the economy. Thus, the national government has had little reason until recently to be concerned with the need for greater fiscal discipline of the types familiar to the states and their political subdivisions. ACIR has recommended that indexing this source of national income, to prevent inflation–driven bracket creep, be continued, and that Congress consider constitutional and legislative provisions requiring a balanced national budget, authorizing the Presidential item veto, and establishing a capital budgeting process. All of these techniques have been used at the state level, and ACIR is currently studying the states' experience for any lessons that might be applied at the national level.[15]

State–Initiated Constitutional Amendments: The Constitution provides a method by which the states may call a new constitutional convention, but such a convention would reopen the whole document to revision, and the fear of so doing has prevented the use of this provision. Congressionally initiated amendments to the Constitution may and do tackle only individual topics. A state–initiated amendment process, similar to the congressional one, would encourage the states to become more active in controlling the national government's tendency to dominate, and would constitute a much needed "gun behind the door," to get the attention of Congress on needed legislation even if the process were seldom used. ACIR has recommended congressional legislation providing for state–called constitutional conventions limited to specific topics.[16]

National Referenda and Initiatives: The Constitution speaks of reserving powers to the states *or to the people*. Yet, there is no provision for the people to act directly on national policy matters. A number of our nation's states have provisions for popular voting to confirm acts of their legislatures (referenda) or to initiate new laws themselves through petition and balloting; and Switzerland also uses this technique a great deal. These twin procedures, if applied at the national level in our nation, could provide a vehicle by which the people themselves could help determine the proper balance between the national and state levels of government.

Reconstitute the Senate: United States Senators originally were appointed by the state legislatures and had a greater obligation to represent the interests of the government as well as the people of their states. This was changed to direct election by the 17th Amendment, but that action removed one of Madison's strongest arguments in *The Federalist*, No. 45, ensuring that state interests would not become subservient to national interests. In West Germany, today, the upper house of the national legislative body is appointed by the German states and, additionally, has the power to veto legislation originated in the lower house, requiring as much as a two-thirds vote of the lower house to override. Obviously, such an arrangement gives the state level much greater political clout on national issues than the American states have today.

Political Parties: The Federal Election Campaign Act places the state and local political parties at a substantial disadvantage, compared to the national parties, in supporting their candidates. This differential treatment weakens the influence of the state and local parties and tends to nationalize the nation's political system. Such a state of affairs damages the dual concept of federalism set forth in the Constitution, and it should be remedied.

National Fiscal Equalization: ACIR's comparative federalism studies have shown that the United States gives considerably less attention than Canada, Australia, or West Germany to establishing equal fiscal capabilities among the states. Without such equalization, the states can be relied upon less, and national programs inevitably result. The primary equalization tool used in the United States at the national level is the general revenue sharing program. That program also is the least intrusive from a policy standpoint. Thus, on two counts, the general revenue sharing program should become the keystone of federal financial assistance to the state and local governments, and other programs increasingly should be merged into broad and flexible block grants distributed through equalizing formulas and limited to essential purposes. If we were to redesign our federal-aid system along these lines, it would assist state and local governments to meet the needs of their own citizens rather than being co-opted as administrators of national programs.

State and Local Performance: A major new initiative by the Advisory Commission on Intergovernmental Relations—in cooperation with the state ACIR's and national public interest groups—might be made as part of the upcoming Constitutional bicentennial celebration, to enhance the performance of state and local governments and to improve the state-local relationships in each of the fifty states. Such an effort would be designed to help these subnational units be more capable of responding to the needs of their own citizens directly, without depending upon national guidance and federal-aid. Our Commission has a substantial amount of technical material that can be shared with the states and their localities, and has been working diligently in the last several years to establish a nationwide network of state ACIR's to carry this work forward.

Judicial Federalism: Finally, ACIR recommended establishing the State-Local Legal Center, and continues to support it. However, the activities of this center need to be stepped up dramatically if the rights of the state and local governments are to be adequately protected in the federal courts. Special efforts, enlisting the talents of the nation's best lawyers, need to be mounted to reverse recent debilitating court decisions on such issues as local antitrust liability and the applicability of federal labor standards to state and local employees.

Conclusion

This list of potential means of restoring balance in our American federal system is not exhaustive. However, it sets forth an appropriate agenda for serious consideration in these next few years leading to the 200th anniversary of our Constitution. I invite a spirited debate on these and other similar proposals.

Notes

1. The following description is drawn largely from David B. Walker, *Toward a Functioning Federalism* (Cambridge, MA: Winthrop Publishers, Inc., 1981), Ch. 2.

2. This section is drawn from David R. Beam, Timothy J. Conlan, and David B. Walker, "Federalism: The Challenge of Conflicting Theories and Contemporary Practice," in Ada W. Finifter, ed., *Political Science: The State of The Discipline* (Washington, D.C.: The American Political Science Association, 1983), 253–256.

3. Advisory Commission on Intergovernmental Relations, *Governmental Functions and Processes: Local and Areawide*, Report A–45 (Washington, D.C.: U.S. Government Printing Office, 1974).

4. Advisory Commission on Intergovernmental Relations, *Studies in Comparative Federalism: Australia, Canada, United States and West Germany*, Report M–130 (Washington, D.C.: U.S. Government Printing Office, November, 1981).

5. This section and the next are based upon Walker, *Toward a Functioning Federalism*, Ch. 3.

6. Advisory Commission on Intergovernmental Relations, *A Crisis of Confidence and Competence*, Report A–77 (Washington, D.C.: U.S. Government Printing Office, July 1980).

7. Ibid., 120–121.

8. Advisory Commission on Intergovernmental Relations, *Categorical Grants: Their Role and Design*, Report A–52 (Washington, D.C.: U.S. Government Printing Office, 1977), Ch. VII.

9. Advisory Commission on Intergovernmental Relations, *Regulatory Federalism: Policy, Process, Impact and Reform*, Report A–95 (Washington D.C.: U.S. Government Printing Office, February 1984).

10. Presidential Task Force on Regulatory Relief, *Reagan Administration Achievements in Regulatory Relief for State and Local*

Government: A Progress Report (Washington, D.C.: The White House, August 1982), 2.

11. City of Lafayette v. Louisiana Power and Light Co., 435 U.S. 419 (1978) and Community Communications Co. Inc. v. City of Boulder, 102 S. Ct. 835 (1982).

12. Advisory Commission on Intergovernmental Relations, *The Question of State Government Capability*, Report A–98 (Washington, D.C.: U.S. Government Printing Office, January 1985); Advisory Commission on Intergovernmental Relations, *State and Local Roles in the Federal System*, Report A–88 (Washington, D.C.: U.S. Government Printing Office, April 1982); Advisory Commission on Intergovernmental Relations, *Measuring Local Discretionary Authority*, Report M–131 (Washington, D.C.: U.S. Government Printing Office, November 1981).

13. Advisory Commission on Intergovernmental Relations, *Regulatory Federalism: Policy, Process, Impact and Reform*, 269.

14. Ibid., 258–259.

15. Advisory Commission on Intergovernmental Relations, *Strengthening the Federal Revenue System: Implications for State and Local Taxing and Borrowing*, Report A–97 (Washington, D.C.: U.S. Government Printing Office, October 1984).

16. Advisory Commission on Intergovernmental Relations, *An Agenda for American Federalism: Restoring Confidence and Competence*, Report A–86 (Washington, D.C.: U.S. Government Printing Office, June 1981), 151–154.

4

Drunk and Disorderly: Canadian Federalism Reels into Its Second Century

EDWIN R. BLACK
Queen's University, Kingston
Canada

I

AN INQUIRY INTO HER FEDERALISM IS ALMOST TANTAmount to a crash course in the whole politics of Canada. In the New World's only constitutional monarchy, most of the major political wars of this half century have been waged within a very peculiar Canadian language—it is the vocabulary of a fiercely fought federalism that few foreign observers can ever follow with confidence. That federalism has just survived a series of political battles as tough as any it has ever faced and it is time to take stock of one of the longest-running constitutional systems in the western world. One reason for doing so is that Canada demonstrates there is more than one desirable and effective way of organizing good government on this continent. Americans may not be in exactly the same boat as Canadians but, as a former prime minister once said, they are both trying to sail in much the same waters.

There may be no more appropriate locus for the inquiry than a venue dedicated to the legacy of George Mason. As the father of the Virginia constitution, he exerted a major influence on the United States Bill of Rights and, with Patrick Henry and many others, he was a fierce opponent of granting large, vaguely-specified powers to governmental authority. The parallels with contemporary Canadian battles about federalism are striking. That said, one must take care with one's comparative interpretations. Analysis that concentrates on the institutional forms of freedom and federalism to the neglect of social setting and political history will founder in ignorance just as surely as the most parochial of inquiries.

What Canada has been up to over the past quarter-century is changing the rules of the federal game, and changing them fairly dramatically. No matter, apparently, that the system seemed to be working fairly well; the engineer's maxim, "if it ain't broke, don't fix it," was totally ignored. Since the early 1960s Canadians have:

a. given substance to their legal independence from Great Britain,
b. instituted official bilingualism in the central government,
c. added new players and referees to the game of politics,
d. turned the Canadian party systems inside outside,
e. grafted a liberal bill of rights on to a traditionalist constitution,
f. shattered the remains of parliamentary and legislative sovereignty, and finally,
g. initiated potentially revolutionary free trade talks with the United States.

It is this potent brew of law and politicking that has given Canadian federalism both the appearance and the reality of being drunk and disorderly as it staggers into its second full century. The prospect is not for more sobriety and predictability but the reverse. The Heisenberg principle of uncertainty has been established as a governing characteristic of Canadian political life for at least a decade.

The politics of Canadian federalism has long emphasized and been shaped by governments—provincial and central. The result has been a self-promoted idea of the country as a series of highly-varied communities, one where no one would feel forced to assimilate himsef to a single national cultural model. Compared with this image of Canada as "a community of communities"—as a former prime minister, Joe Clark, put it—is a picture of the United States as a society dominated by a semi-official ideology of aggressive individualism. While the contrast is somewhat overdrawn, Americans do have reinforcement of that individualism by an extraordinarily influential Bill of Rights and by judicial interpretations which resulted in the installation of well-heeled individual and corporate interests as exercisers of major influence in the constitutional development of United States federalism.

Today, despite all the early constitutional engineering, it is Canada's system rather than the federalism of the once-revolutionary United States of America which is the more varied and decentralized. That is only one of a series of ironies that comes springing at you once you start probing federalism on a comparative basis. The ironies result from the hammering out of founding idealisms on the anvils of youthful development and political maturity.

Consider. Americans took their constitutional ideals from an age still in transition from the remnants of feudalism to the promises of liberal individualism. They invented modern federalism. Why? To keep the hungry beast of far-off government authority in leash, to make sure it could never get enough power to harm the people. Unrelenting opposition to centralization of political authority—whether in Britain or in far-off national capitals— that was to be the key to American liberty. Federalism was an important part of the combination lock. Today, however, people in the American national capital exercise the greatest concentration of military, economic, and political power the world has ever seen. While American federalism provides a convenient degree of administrative decentralization, it offers only the most feeble of barriers to the persuasive centralization of Washington and its moneybags.

Canada's federal constitutionalism was developed in a different atmosphere—in reaction to two major happenings of the nineteenth century. First came the often bloody and usually unsuccessful liberal revolutions of nineteenth century Europe. Mobs everywhere were screaming for democracy and individual freedom. Generally, what they delivered was near-anarchy instead. Second, and most important for Canada, came the American Civil War. For the Fathers of the Canadian Confederation that was proof positive of the dangers brought by the excesses of unbridled democracy and federal decentralization of authority. It was in an effort to avoid such troubles that a highly centralizing constitutional document was drafted—the British North America Act of 1867. As it happened, the working out of a different destiny brought Canada the diversity of communities and thriving federal *system* of government and politics that the Americans had once sought for themselves.

II

Canada's federalism has been much studied. There seems little need to review its first century of development; it has been well-documented. Turn instead to 1968 and the accession of Pierre Elliot Trudeau to power. Besides providing plentiful copy for Sunday newspapers everywhere, Trudeau installed a technocratic elite in the central government, raised French to equal status with English as a working language in the federal public service, smashed the British constitutional connection with a wholly domestic amending process, and, by force of political will and skill, imposed on the federation something else it had never had before: a constitutionally-entrenched Charter of Rights and Freedoms [sections 1-34, Constitution Act of 1982; see appendix for complete text of Act]. This last was the most significant. The American Bill of Rights exerted such immense influence on the development of United States federalism, that its Canadian analogue demands the close attention of all those who would understand Confederation today.

Not everybody has applauded enactment of the Canadian Charter. Although its virtues are generally taken for granted, they are not nearly as numerous as popularly supposed. Most politicians were, of course, forced into line— some of them with great reluctance. The popular picture of the Charter is so unbalanced, in its favor, that the ensuing discussion has been deliberately tilted in the opposite direction. The reader has been warned. Unlike politicians, academics who dissent from the sacred virtues of the Charter can rely on Adlai Stevenson's definition of a free society as one in which it is safe to be unpopular. Of particular interest here are the questionable effects of the 1982 changes on the federal qualities and constitutional practices of the Canadian political system.

It is with some justice that the Charter has been called "the most radical break ever made with a constitutional and legal order hitherto characterized by continuity and incremental development."[1] Why? Because, as Professor D. A. Schmeiser told one conference, in locking a particular set of rights away behind doors closed to the political process, the Charter would be destructive to Canada's federal system. Entrenchment of rights acts as a brake on necessary social experimentation and change "because a final court tends to express a uniform social philosophy, tends to disallow imaginative solutions to social ills, and tends to prefer consistency over provincial diversity."[2]

Debate about the best way to enhance, guarantee, and protect civil liberties in Canada revolves around different conceptions of and beliefs in the constitutional system developed from the British political inheritance and domestic practice. The legal and political systems are essentially in conflict and produce a system of government that lacks the coherence of either the British or the American varieties. The 1982 Charter made the problem even worse by trying to combine the strength of each without first resolving their practical, theoretical, and traditional differences. The shortcomings of the constitutional instrument are many—whether considered from the perspective of comparable legislation in other countries, from the viewpoint of legal interpretation, or in terms of the various attempts to formulate constitutional resolution of disputes which had proved impossible to resolve politically. One of the central difficulties in drafting any bill of rights is that on the one side it must employ quite general statements—which by their nature tend to be vague, while on the other side it must manage to comprehend the specific concerns of both the drafters and their constituents—which by their nature are not vague. The new Canadian legislation did not manage the successful compromise that was required.

Some have argued that not only is the entrenched Charter illusory as a guarantee of fundamental rights and freedoms, but that underlying the whole notion is a political and economic theory that the minimal state is constitutionally desirable—a proposition which is far from agreed upon in Canada. Whether they have seen this in the document or not, too many commentators have joined in discussing the Charter as though it were a constitutional import of pure liberal individualism. This it is not. It is an unstable mixture of individual and collectivist or corporative concerns. For evidence of the latter, one need look only at the linguistic group rights [sections 16–22], the maintenance of minority group educational privilege [section 23], aboriginal rights [sections 25, 35], protection for high unemployment sectors [sections 6 (4), 36], the provisions for favorable discrimination projects [sections 6 (4), 15 (2)], the rights extended by implication to corporations,[3] and the escape hatches of the "demonstrably justified" [section 1] and "notwithstanding" [section 33] clauses. In the American case, some of the concerns represented by these phrases were comprehended by the concepts involved in "states' rights" which were effectively emasculated by later amendment and interpretation[4] R. St. J. Macdonald has pointed out that the first ten amendments to the United States Constitution function as they do because of "complementary constellations in their legal universe," provisions which are missing from the Canadian scene. He has gone on to observe that experience elsewhere "confirms not only that the rights enumerated in entrenched Charters tend to be time specific, but also that entrenchment has a prophylactic effect on the recognition of new rights," especially as the "inclusion or exclusion of certain rights often has no basis other than historical accident or political expediency."[5] In his concurring opinion, Smiley argued that "the debate on the Charter emphasized special claims rather than those rights possessed by all Canadians, and in particular there was relatively little debate on what the Charter itself designates as 'fundamental freedoms.'"[6]

Smiley and J. A. Corry have claimed that the Charter could have only negative effects on Canadian unity. The way in which the Special Joint Committee of the Senate and House [created to study the patriation issue and hold a series of public hearings] heard the claims of only a few special interests undermined the democratic requirement of a full hearing for all affected parties. Corry thought that the "concentration of politicians, legislatures and public debate on the rival claims of diverse interests keeps our attention riveted on matters much more likely to divide us than to draw us together."[7] The result was a document that "is an inherently fragmenting rather than unifying measure ... [since] the defence of rights centres on conflict rather than cooperation."[8]

Andre Tremblay argued that the Charter contains a "collective rights" orientation that "is the product of confrontation and means fewer collective rights, less justice for minorities, and more bitterness in Quebec. There will also be more confrontation." To a claim that between individual rights and "group rights" there need be no conflict, Tremblay has replied that in Quebec, "the feeling is that individual rights have been used as a weapon to diminish collective rights."[9]

Recognition of this conflict leads to the strongest argument made by critics of the Charter: that collective rights are ultimately within the realm of social policy and ought to be in the purview of Parliament. As S.J.R. Noel observes: "It is not realistic to think that [rights] can somehow be taken out of the Canadian political process. Yet that process revolves around, and is driven by, collective concerns with the politics of accommodation between collectives. If that is the case, where in that process will the Charter of

Rights fit?"[10] Some businessmen and their spokesmen tried to make much of their future vulnerability because of the omission of specific property rights from the Charter. Little notice has been given, however, to what appears to be a significant extension of anti-government protection to the private corporate sphere. The so-called Diefenbaker Bill of Rights of the early sixties limited its protections to human persons. It has now been superceded by entrenched provisions that are being judicially interpreted to extend rights to corporations that may well be "individuals" in a legal sense but are certainly not human.[11] Such is the jurisdictional responsibility for business and commerce in this country that judicial limitations on government arising from such cases will undoubtedly bear most heavily and obviously on provincial policy and activities.

A time of great uncertainty has descended on the federation. No longer is it generally understood which rights are defensible, how they are defined, or from which governments we will be protected on which occasion. As changing social circumstances called for it, Canada's federal arrangements were brought into line by the political arts of skillful negotiation and compromise. Where previously economic and social change were the motors for changes in federalism, now that impulsion will come ever-increasingly from the courts as they try to make legal and constitutional sense of the new legal arrangements. The result is a loss in both popular accountability and flexible response. As Professor Smiley asserts, the Charter

> imposes on the courts—the institutions of the governmental system most attuned towards incrementalism—the major responsibility for effecting this rupture with the past.... It will take decades, or even longer, for the courts to give authoritative meaning to the general phrases of the Charter. It is honeycombed with terms new to jurisprudence in Canada and elsewhere.... Besides giving authoritative meaning to such terms, the courts must define standards of governmental conduct concerning, for example, legal rights and fundamental freedoms where hitherto Parliament and the premiers acting within their own sphere of legislative jurisdiction were supreme.[12]

It could even be found that the entrenched charter does not really guarantee very much by way of rights at all.[13] As Professor Peter Russell has suggested, what Canada has given itself may be only "a particular way of making decisions about rights in which the judicial branch of government has a much more systematic and authoritative role." Such an outcome would mean the society had crippled itself with a political system limited to using but a single methodology—that of judicial decision making—as a means of dealing with a variety of public problems for which a variety of mechanisms might very well prove more effective.[14] The absence of specific guidance to the courts means that it will be a long time indeed before rights can be meaningfully guaranteed.

The plethora of cases launched since 1982 (and particularly since April 1985 and the coming into effect of the equality provisions)[15] is ample testimony to the breadth of plausible legal interpretations.[16] Traditionally, Canadian courts have limited themselves to judgments of fact, trying to avoid the kinds of judgments on law and jurisprudence that characterize the United States system. But the new clauses are changing all this. As the courts are asked to define, apply, and limit the Charter, they are essentially charged with deciding the meaning of fundamental rights as set out in general words of varying and uncertain content. Professor Schmeiser argues that decisions as to the meanings of such words "primarily involve matters of social policy, better left to the legislative process than to the courts." The structure of legal procedure does not complement the formulation of social policy. "The adversary system of judicial proceedings, restricted to the facts of a particular case and limited by rules of evidence and procedure, is ill-equipped to create universal solutions to complex social problems," and particularly in the complex milieu of Canadian federalism.[17]

III

The Charter was said to be neutral toward the federal division of powers because it restrains both types of government. This is not so because the Charter's limitation of provincial powers is actually much greater. That is significant because the services Canadians receive from governments come primarily from those at the provincial and local level. The serious limitations may be found primarily in four areas.

(a) The scope of "property and civil rights" included in the British North America Act [section 92 (13)] is quite different from the wording of the Charter of Rights and Freedoms. The absence of any specific reference to property in the Charter could be particularly disruptive if the legal interpretation of the Charter were to differ radically from tradition. This absence may create very different legal, and perhaps social, relations between citizens, between individuals and groups, and between individuals and the state. Always in some dispute, the "property and civil rights" phrase and the legislative authority it conveys on the provinces are rendered by the Charter of Rights even vaguer and more capable of legal challenge than before.

(b) Provincial administration of justice and procedural uniformities to be required by courts. We can have no idea what these will be because not only is there no general "due process" clause as it is known in United States constitutional law, but there is a reference to "the principles of fundamental justice" [section 7], a phrase which entirely lacks any present judicial definition and is presumably to be distinguished from 'natural justice' which does have agreed legal meanings.

(c) The operation of the equality clauses [section 15 (1,2)] will likely invalidate a host of programs through which provincial governments express their individual tailoring of Canadian realities to suit local communities.

(d) Unlike the American, Australian, or West German situations, in the Canadian federation the provinces have neither voice nor institutional spokesmen like senators to express their views on central lawmaking— whatever its effect on provincial governments.

Although they may not be immediately relevant for the federalist aspects of the working political system, two other points should be noted about the Charter. First is the problem of Clause 1. It subjects all the rights and freedoms in the Charter (save probably for sexual equality) to "such reasonable limits prescribed by law as can be demonstrably justified in a free and democratic society." Here no citizen need apologize for ignorance of the law for the idea is itself a stranger to our jurisprudence. The Supreme Court has been left to work it out, painstaking case by painful case. Second, any legislature which is so determined can pass legislation exempting its operation from interference by significant sectors of the Charter—the infamous "notwithstanding" clauses. Two provincial governments have already taken this course. Quebec made a blanket declaration as a matter of principle in 1982 and the Saskatchewan legislature exempted a "back to work" labor law in 1986.[18]

The central government has also not only indicated its plans but has actually begun playing an active financial part in assisting citizens to put public laws—provincial as well as federal—to the legal test of the Charter. Not much has yet come of this. Should it develop further, though, the practice would give a radically new dimension to intergovernmental relations in Canada and pose a significant threat to the balance of contending forces among the powers of the center and those of the various peripheries. The provincial ability to opt out of future amendments [section 38 (3)] raises the possibility of somewhat different *federal* rights in different provinces.

The *process* of arriving at the amending formula—even if not the amending provisions themselves—is sometimes said to have radically altered Quebec's *de facto* status in the Canadian federation. The point is debatable. That province has probably never had any substantially different formal status in bringing about federal structure amendments than any other province. Its strong position derived from moral and political considerations, not the formal legal ones. Ironically, despite both the outcome of the 1980 "sovereignty–association" referendum vote in Quebec and the 1984 national election defeat of the Liberal party, its long–time protector–party in Ottawa, *l'ancienne province* has lost none of its political and moral weight. It seems simply to have shifted its instrument at the federal capital from the Liberal to the Progressive Conservative party, at least temporarily. Prime Minister Brian Mulroney's attempt to bring the Parti Québécois' successor, the Quebec government of Liberal Robert Bourassa, into some agreement with the 1982 document is more symbolic politically than constitutionally meaningful.

The Act does strengthen the traditional importance of provincial governments in the amending process by:

1. explicit constitutional provisions (provincial participation in general amendments not legally required previously) [sections 38–49], and,
2. Abolishing unilateral changes to the basic structure brought about by the federal government.

IV

The constitutional exercise during the early 1980s changed the eligibility rules for playing in Canadian politics. Two new teams have been promoted from the minors to the majors. After a short run one of those teams–the native peoples who managed to gain some quasi–political status at the constitutional talks—will probably face relegation at the end of this season. Not so with the other team, the private sector: they will be around for a while now. That is because litigating the meaning of the 1982 Charter allows a whole new set of actors to buy their way into what used to be a purely political decision–making process. That process, of course, has been transformed by the elevation of the courts to enormously greater status and the translation into the legal sphere of many disputes which were once the exclusive quarreling property of governments and politicians. It is worth noting that the public, in whose interest this business was all allegedly being arranged, was never asked in any way—by vote, referendum or general election—to indicate whether it approved of the bargains struck among the politicians and special interest groups. Neither was serious attempt made in these constitutional "add-ons" to provide the Canadian federation either with a federal Senate or a regionally-significant form of popular representation.

Despite all this constitutionalizing, it can be argued that developments other than formal legal amendment are at least equally responsible for contemporary changes in Canadian federalism. Two of those developments are the secessionist referendum of 1978 in Quebec and radical party political change at the federal level.

Not for nothing has Canada been called "The Peaceable Kingdom." Most other states in the world would use the word treason for attempts to divide and dismember the state. The United States fought a civil war over an earlier secessionist attempt. In Canada a separatist party not only pursued the goal legally for many years but was allowed to win electoral control of one of the most important governments, and hold a referendum on the subject. Throughout anglophone Canada there was an almost universal assumption that military force would not be used to keep Quebec within the federation if a majority of her people decided they wished to leave. Surely this willingness to allow the peaceful dismantling of the state constitutes "impressive testimony to the civility and tolerance" of the society involved. As Alan Cairns has said, further, "in a constitutional sense this contributes to the norm that the Canadian political system is ultimately based on the freely given consent of its population, defined both provincially and nationally."

For many years, the National Liberal Federation of Canada was thought to be the country's natural governing party. It ruled from the 1920s until last year with only four interruptions. We can now see, though, that the year 1958 marked the beginning of the end of Liberal party hegemony in Canada; the old coalition fell apart. Lester Pearson's minority governments in the sixties never managed to put the coalition together again. When he had the chance during the seventies, Pierre Trudeau apparently did not care to try. He allowed the Progressive Conservatives to become the sole legitimate spokesmen for most of the west and the east against the centralizing middle in Ottawa. Their many years in the wilderness had transformed the Conservatives into a party that not only preached but believed in the virtues of a truly decentralist, federal system. Their first six months in office after September 1984 were devoted to a whole series of measures to assuage the long-burning anger of the provincial communities against the center. Within twelve months, however, the honeymoon had ended and the country's eleven governments were at odds with each other once again. Potentially the most corrosive issue of all for Canada's federalism in the eighties is the central government's ambition to negotiate a wide range of freer trade arrangements with the United States.

Whatever their long-term ambitions or tendencies, the Progressive Conservative regime in Ottawa must govern under political conditions very different from those which once prevailed. No longer can Ottawa dip into a deep purse to buy its way out of policy or jurisdictional disputes with provincial governments. Its incentive for doing so rested largely with perceptions of the relative division of citizen loyalties toward the provincial and central governments. Mr. Trudeau's Charter of Rights and Freedoms was designed to help restore the central government as a focus of stronger citizen loyalty—at the expense of the provinces. Where once there might have been generous subsidies, citizens can now look to Ottawa with gratitude for a radically strengthened court system and the Charter of Rights and Freedoms. To the cynic, law seems but thin compensation. It is in the longer run, however, that we must look for possible achievement of that particular objective of Mr. Trudeau.

In the meantime, Canadians who once enjoyed a wide range of effective freedoms under a traditional regime must wait, and see, and litigate, to discover what their rights and freedoms amount to in the last part of this century. Coping with frustrated citizen hopes will be a chore for both orders of government in the Canadian federation. Of equal significance with these matters is another. That is the translation of a host of major public conflicts from the political arena where accommodation is the watch word to the zero–sum game of the legal arena where winners take all and the losers have to lump it.

Before he entered elective politics, Pierre Trudeau was an embattled fighter against political arbitrariness, an intellectual liberal, and a serious student of federalism. During his time in the federal prime ministry, he acquired a deserved reputation as a man who prized clarity, rationality, and an anti–nationalist form of federalism. He it was who insisted on driving through the recent constitutional changes—whether most people wanted them or not. Then, in mid–1984 he resigned from office. Now we may ask what has been his legacy for Canadian federalism?

It is clearly a mixed blessing at best. Even if these cloudy skies do have a silver lining, we must agree with Don Marquis that it's hard to get that kind of silver to the mint. Although Trudeau's Official Languages Act[19] strained the federation enormously, the gains for the country's self–understanding and political coherence are surely indisputable. From the Charter exercise itself there are some other gains. The agenda of public issues has finally been relieved of that enormous triviality—patriating the constitution. More importantly, governnent arbitrariness is facing some new checks.[20]

But the liabilities loom larger. The consecration of one set of values as higher than all others in the realm opens up a whole new ground of contention for factions to demand that their pet principles be given loftier status. The charter that does this also gives corporations new powers with which to browbeat weaker provinces into acquiescence. The cohesion of the Quebec francophone group has been weakened. A whole raft of vague and confused legalist impedimenta has been fastened about the neck of a largely traditionalist constitution. Most obvious of all, the country now faces at least ten years of uncertainty and confusion—uncertainty about how the courts will reconstruct our federal polity, uncertainty about what citizens may reasonably expect of government, and complete confusion as to which of the various federal governments is probably responsible for it.

The 1982 changes add up to a simmering legal revolution for the judicial system. Whether they will wreak comparable changes in the federal aspects of the system remains to be revealed by the course of judicial activity over the next few years. Although little discussed so far, we must remember that in the past it has been the policies of the central government—and not formal constitutional changes—which have been far more influential in determining the real character of Canada's federalism. That this will continue to be the case is suggested by the developments relating to budget-cutting, regional economic stimulation, and petroleum exploitation during the first two years of Brian Mulroney's government.

In constitutional perspective, then, the Canadian ship of state can be seen to be staggering along in considerable disorder. The ship's compass is badly out of whack, inexperienced helmsmen have been impressed from the bar, and new navigation charts are being patched together on the spot. Whatever the perils, the country is now lumbered with these new methods of bringing about change. The old system has been discredited. As in the United States, the growing judicialization of public questions conspires with mass-mediated cynicism to cripple the unfashionable but sturdy engine of political process on which Canada relied for more than a century to work its way through many troubled waters.

Notes

1. D. V. Smiley, "A Dangerous Deed: The Constitution Act, 1982," in Keith Banting and Richard Simeon, eds., *And No One Cheered: Federalism, Democracy and The Constitution Act* (Toronto: Methuen, 1983), 89.

2. D. A. Schmeiser, "Entrenchment Revisited: The Effect of the Charter of Rights and Freedoms," in W. R. McKercher, ed., *The U. S. Bill of Rights and the Canadian Charter of Rights and Freedoms* (Toronto: Ontario Economic Council, 1983), 168.

3. [While corporations are not given specific rights in the Constitution Act, 1982, judicial interpretations of the "corporate person" could expand many rights granted to "persons."]

4. [In contrast to the Canadian approach, note Elazar's description of the American view of group rights.]

5. R. A. Macdonald, "Postscript and Prelude – The Jurisprudence of the Charter: Eight Theses," in E. P. Belobaba and E. Gertner, eds., *The New Constitution and the Charter of Rights: Fundamental Issues and Strategies*. A Special Symposium Edition of the Supreme Court Law Review (Toronto: Butterworths, 1983), 338, 325.

6. Smiley in Banting and Simeon, *And No One Cheered*, 81.

7. J. A. Corry quoted by Smiley in Banting and Simeon, *And No One Cheered*, 81.

8. Smiley in Banting and Simeon, *And No One Cheered*, 80–81.

9. See "Rights and Constitutional Change in Canada: A Roundtable Discussion," in McKercher, *U.S. Bill of Rights*, 142, 145–146. See also Macdonald in Belobaba and Gertner, *New Constitution*.

10. "Rights and Constitutional Change," in McKercher, *U.S. Bill of Rights*, 144.

11. See, for example, Hunter v. Southam Inc. (1984) 2 SCR 145; William D. Moull, "Business Law Implications of the Canadian Charter of Rights and Freedoms," *Canadian Business Law*

Journal 8 (1983–1984) : 449–484; and Gordon F. Henderson and Emilio S. Binavince, "Doing Business in Canada and the Judicial Review of Wrongful Government Statutory and Regulatory Action," *Canada–U.S. Law Journal* 7 (1984) : 1–60. See also Linda McQuaig, "Business may benefit most from Charter of Rights," *The Globe and Mail*, Toronto, 5 January 1985, sec. Bl.

12. Smiley in Banting and Simeon, *And No One Cheered*, 89–90.

13. See "Labor movement discovers Charter is a two–edged sword," *The Globe and Mail*, Toronto, 29 July 1985, sec. B3.

14. P. H. Russell, "The Effect of a Charter of Rights on the Policymaking Role of Canadian Courts," *Canadian Public Administration* 25 (1982) : 29,32.

15. [Section 32 (2) delayed the effective date of the equality provisions (section 15) until three years after the Charter came into force.]

16. See, for example, the following range of decisions: Law Society of Upper Canada v. Skapinker (1984) 1 SCR 375; A.–G. Quebec v. Protestant School Boards (1984) 2 SCR 66; Hunter v. Southam Inc. (1984) 2 SCR 145; Singh et. al. v. Minister of Employment and Immigration (1985) 1 SCR 177; R. v. Big M Drug Mart Ltd. et. al. (1985) 1 SCR 295; Plantation Indoor Plants Ltd. v. A.–G. Alberta (1985) 1 SCR 366; Operation Dismantle Inc. et. al. v. The Queen, et. al. (1985) 1 SCR 441; R. v. Therens et. al. (1985) 1 SCR 613; and Rahn v. The Queen (1985) 1 SCR 659.

17. Schmeiser, in McKercher, *U.S. Bill of Rights*, 165.

18. It can be argued that altogether these omissions place any effective guarantee of human liberties in more jeopardy than they might have been before. However valid that might be, less credence can be given to the criticism against the Charter that it would have forestalled neither Mr. Trudeau's imposition of emergency, wartime powers in 1970 (allegedly directed against Quebec terrorists) nor the mistreatment of Japanese–Canadians during World War II. Even the most liberally–minded countries do not let

bills of rights stand in the way of state–threatening "national emergencies."

19. [The Official Languages Act of 1969 guaranteed the equal status of English and French as the official languages of Canada for all Parliamentary and governmental purposes.]

20. The reasoning used in three cases cited above (Hunter v. Southam, Singh, and Operation Dismantle), if not the actual decisions, foreshadows much closer judicial surveillance of the political executive than has ever been the case in Canada before.

Appendix A
The Virginia Declaration of Rights

[12 June 1776]

A Declaration of Rights made by the Representatives of the good people of Virginia, assembled in full and free Convention; which rights do pertain to them and their posterity, as the basis and foundation of Government.

1. That all men are by nature equally free and independent, and have certain inherent rights, of which, when they enter into a state of society, they cannot, by any compact, deprive or divest their posterity; namely, the enjoyment of life and liberty, with the means of acquiring and possessing property, and pursuing and obtaining happiness and safety.

2. That all power is vested in, and consequently derived from, the People; that magistrates are their trustees and servants, and at all times amenable to them.

3. That Government is, or ought to be, instituted for the common benefit, protection, and security of the people, nation, or community;—of all the various modes and forms of Government that is best which is capable of producing the greatest degree of happiness and safety, and is most effectually secured against the danger of mal–administration;—and that, whenever any Government shall be found inadequate or contrary to these purposes, a majority of the community hath an indubitable, unalienable, and indefeasible right, to reform, alter, or abolish it, in such manner as shall be judged most conducive to the publick weal.

4. That no man, or set of men, are entitled to exclusive or separate emoluments and privileges from the community, but in consideration of publick services; which, not being descendible, neither ought the offices of Magistrate, Legislator, or Judge, to be hereditary.

5. That the Legislative and Executive powers of the State should be separate and distinct from the Judicative; and, that the members of the two first may be restrained from oppression, by feeling and participating the burdens of the people, they should, at fixed periods, be reduced to a private station, return into that body from which they were originally taken, and the vacancies be supplied by frequent, certain, and regular elections, in which all, or any part of the former members, to be again eligible, or ineligible, as the law shall direct.

6. That elections of members to serve as Representatives of the people, in Assembly, ought to be free; and that all men, having sufficient evidence of permanent common interest with, and attachment to, the community, have the right of suffrage, and cannot be taxed or deprived of their property for publick uses without their own consent or that of their Representative so elected, nor bound by any law to which they have not, in like manner, assented, for the publick good.

7. That all power of suspending laws, or the execution of laws, by any authority, without consent of the Representatives of the people, is injurious to their rights, and ought not to be exercised.

8. That in all capital or criminal prosecutions a man hath a right to demand the cause and nature of his accusation, to be confronted with the accusers and witnesses, to call for evidence in his favour, and to a speedy trial by an impartial jury of his vicinage, without whose unanimous consent he cannot be found guilty, nor can he be compelled to give evidence against himself; that no man be deprived of his liberty except by the law of the land, or the judgment of his peers.

9. That excessive bail ought not to be required, nor excessive fines imposed, nor cruel and unusual punishments inflicted.

10. That general warrants, whereby any officer or messenger may be commanded to search suspected places without evidence of a fact committed, or to seize any person or persons not named, or whose offence is not particularly described and supported by evidence, are grievous and oppressive, and ought not to be granted.

11. That in controversies respecting property, and in suits between man and man, the ancient trial by Jury is preferable to any other, and ought to be held sacred.

12. That the freedom of the Press is one of the greatest bulwarks of liberty, and can never be restrained but by despotick Governments.

13. That a well-regulated Militia, composed of the body of the people, trained to arms, is the proper, natural, and safe defence of a free State; that Standing Armies, in time of peace, should be avoided as dangerous to liberty; and that, in all cases, the miltary should be under strict subordination to, and governed by, the civil power.

14. That the people have a right to uniform Government; and, therefore, that no Government separate from, or independent of, the Government of Virginia, ought to be erected or established within the limits thereof.

15. That no free Government, or the blessing of liberty, can be preserved to any people but by a firm adherence to justice, moderation, temperance, frugality, and virtue, and by frequent recurrence to fundamental principles.

16. That Religion, or the duty which we owe to our Creator, and the manner of discharging it, can be directed only by reason and conviction, not by force or violence; and, therefore, all men are equally entitled to the free exercise of religion, according to the dictates of conscience; and that it is the mutual duty of all to practise Christian forbearance, love, and charity, towards each other.

Appendix B
The Constitution Act, 1982

The Schedule to The Constitution Act, 1982, "Modernization of the Constitution," has been omitted, as have annotations referring to such past acts as the British North America Act of 1867, now referred to as The Constitution Act, 1867.

Part I

Canadian Charter of Rights and Freedoms

Whereas Canada is founded upon principles that recognize the supremacy of God and the rule of law:

Guarantee of Rights and Freedoms

1. The Canadian Charter of Rights and Freedoms guarantees the rights and freedoms set out in it subject only to such reasonable limits prescribed by law as can be demonstrably justified in a free and democratic society.

Fundamental Freedoms

2. Everyone has the following fundamental freedoms:

(a) freedom of conscience and religion;
(b) freedom of thought, belief, opinion and expression, including freedom of the press and other media of communication;
(c) freedom of peaceful assembly; and
(d) freedom of association.

Democratic Rights

3. Every citizen of Canada has the right to vote in an election of members of the House of Commons or of a legislative assembly and to be qualified for membership therein.

4. (1) No House of Commons and no legislative assembly shall continue for longer than five years from the date fixed for the return of the writs of a general election of its members.

(2) In time of real or apprehended war, invasion or insurrection, a House of Commons may be continued by Parliament and a legislative assembly may be continued by the legislature beyond five years if such continuation is not opposed by the votes of more than one-third of the members of the House of Commons or the legislative assembly, as the case may be.

5. There shall be a sitting of Parliament and of each legislature at least once every twelve months.

Mobility Rights

6. (1) Every citizen of Canada has the right to enter, remain in and leave Canada.

(2) Every citizen of Canada and every person who has the status of a permanent resident of Canada has the right
(a) to move to and take up residence in any province; and
(b) to pursue the gaining of a livelihood in any province.

(3) The rights specified in subsection (2) are subject to
(a) any laws or practices of general application in force in a province other than those that discriminate among persons pri-

marily on the basis of province of present or previous residence; and

(b) any laws providing for reasonable residency requirements as a qualifiction for the receipt of publicly provided social services.

(4) Subsections (2) and (3) do not preclude any law, program or activity that has as its object the amelioration in a province of conditions of individuals in that province who are socially or economically disadvantaged if the rate of employment in that province is below the rate of employment in Canada.

Legal Rights

7. Everyone has the right to life, liberty and security of the person and the right not to be deprived thereof except in accordance with the principles of fundamental justice.

8. Everyone has the right to be secure against unreasonable search or seizure.

9. Everyone has the right not to be arbitrarily detained or imprisoned.

10. Everyone has the right on arrest or detention

(a) to be informed promptly of the reasons therefor;

(b) to retain and instruct counsel without delay and to be informed of that right; and

(c) to have the validity of the detention determined by way of *habeas corpus* and to be released if the detention is not lawful.

11. Any person charged with an offence has the right

(a) to be informed without unreasonable delay of the specific offence;

(b) to be tried within a reasonable time;

(c) not to be compelled to be a witness in proceedings against that person in respect of the offence;

(d) to be presumed innocent until proven guilty according to law in a fair and public hearing by an independent and impartial tribunal;

(e) not to be denied reasonable bail without just cause;

(f) except in the case of an offence under military law tried before a military tribunal, to the benefit of trial by jury where the maximum punishment for the offence is imprisonment for five years or a more severe punishment;
(g) not to be found guilty on account of any act or omission unless, at the time of the act or omission, it constituted an offence under Canadian or international law or was criminal according to the general principles of law recognized by the community of nations;
(h) if finally acquitted of the offence, not to be tried for it again and, if finally found guilty and punished for the offence, not to be tried or punished for it again; and
(i) if found guilty of the offence and if the punishment for the offence has been varied between the time of commission and the time of sentencing, to the benefit of the lesser punishment.

12. Everyone has the right not to be subjected to any cruel and unusual treatment or punishment.

13. A witness who testifies in any proceedings has the right not to have any incriminating evidence so given used to incriminate that witness in any other proceedings, except in a prosecution for perjury or for the giving of contradictory evidence.

14. A party or witness in any proceedings who does not understand or speak the language in which the proceedings are conducted or who is deaf has the right to the assistance of an interpreter.

Equality Rights

15. (1) Every individual is equal before and under the law and has the right to the equal protection and equal benefit of the law without discrimination and, in particular, without discrimination based on race, national or ethnic origin, colour, religion, sex, age or mental or physical disability.

(2) Subsection (1) does not preclude any law, program or activity that has as its object the amelioration of conditions of disadvan-

taged individuals or groups including those that are disadvantaged because of race, national or ethnic origin, colour, religion, sex, age or mental or physical disability.

Official Languages of Canada

16. (1) English and French are the official languages of Canada and have equality of status and equal rights and privileges as to their use in all institutions of the Parliament and government of Canada.

(2) English and French are the official languages of New Brunswick and have equality of status and equal rights and privileges as to their use in all institutions of the legislature and government of New Brunswick.

(3) Nothing in this Charter limits the authority of Parliament or a legislature to advance the equality of status or use of English and French.

17. (1) Everyone has the right to use English or French in any debates and other proceedings of Parliament.

(2) Everyone has the right to use English or French in any debates and other proceedings of the legislature of New Brunswick.

18. (1) The statutes, records and journals of Parliament shall be printed and published in English and French and both language versions are equally authoritative.

(2) The statutes, records and journals of the legislature of New Brunswick shall be printed and published in English and French and both language versions are equally authoritative.

19. (1) Either English or French may be used by any person in, or in any pleading in or process issuing from, any court established by Parliament.

(2) Either English or French may be used by any person in, or in any pleading in or process issuing from, any court of New Brunswick.

20. (1) Any member of the public in Canada has the right to communicate with, and to receive available services from, any

head or central office of an institution of the Parliament or government of Canada in English or French, and has the same right with respect to any other office of any such institution where

(a) there is a significant demand for communications with and services from that office in such language; or

(b) due to the nature of the office, it is reasonable that communications with and services from that office be available in both English and French.

(2) Any member of the public in New Brunswick has the right to communicate with, and to receive available services from, any office of an institution of the legislature or government of New Brunswick in English or French.

21. Nothing in sections 16 to 20 abrogates or derogates from any right, privilege or obligation with respect to the English and French languages, or either of them, that exists or is continued by virtue of any other provision of the Constitution of Canada.

22. Nothing in sections 16 to 20 abrogates or derogates from any legal or customary right or privilege acquired or enjoyed either before or after the coming into force of this Charter with respect to any language that is not English or French.

Minority Language Educational Rights

23. (1) Citizens of Canada

(a) whose first language learned and still understood is that of the English or French linguistic minority population of the province in which they reside, or

(b) who have received their primary school instruction in Canada in English or French and reside in a province where the language in which they received that instruction is the language of the English or French linguistic minority population of the province,

have the right to have their children receive primary and secondary school instruction in that language in that province.

(2) Citizens of Canada of whom any child has received or is receiving primary or secondary school instruction in English or French in Canada, have the right to have all their children receive primary and secondary school instruction in the same language.

(3) The right of citizens of Canada under subsections (1) and (2) to have their children receive primary and secondary school instruction in the language of the English or French linguistic minority population of a province

(a) applies wherever in the province the number of children of citizens who have such a right is sufficient to warrant the provision to them out of public funds of minority language instruction; and

(b) includes, where the number of those children so warrants, the right to have them receive that instruction in minority language educational facilities provided out of public funds.

Enforcement

24. (1) Anyone whose rights or freedoms, as guaranteed by this Charter, have been infringed or denied may apply to a court of competent jurisdiction to obtain such remedy as the court considers appropriate and just in the circumstances.

(2) Where, in proceedings under subsection (1), a court concludes that evidence was obtained in a manner that infringed or denied any rights or freedoms guaranteed by this Charter, the evidence shall be excluded if it is established that, having regard to all the circumstances, the admission of it in the proceedings would bring the administration of justice into disrepute.

General

25. The guarantee in this Charter of certain rights and freedoms shall not be construed so as to abrogate or derogate from any aboriginal, treaty or other rights or freedoms that pertain to the aboriginal peoples of Canada including

(a) any rights or freedoms that have been recognized by the Royal Proclamation of October 7, 1763; and

(b) any rights or freedoms that may be acquired by the aboriginal peoples of Canada by way of land claims settlement.

26. The guarantee in this Charter of certain rights and freedoms shall not be construed as denying the existence of any other rights or freedoms that exist in Canada.

27. This Charter shall be interpreted in a manner consistent with the preservation and enhancement of the multicultural heritage of Canadians.

28. Notwithstanding anything in this Chapter, the rights and freedoms referred to in it are guaranteed equally to male and female persons.

29. Nothing in this Charter abrogates or derogates from any rights or privileges guaranteed by or under the Constitution of Canada in respect of denominational, separate or dissentient schools.

30. A reference in this Charter to a Province or to the legislative assembly or legislature of a province shall be deemed to include a reference to the Yukon Territory and the Northwest Territories, or to the appropriate legislative authority thereof, as the case may be.

31. Nothing in this Charter extends the legislative powers of any body or authority.

Application of Charter

32. (1) This Charter applies

(a) to the Parliament and goverment of Canada in respect of all matters within the authority of Parliament including all matters relating to the Yukon Territory and Northwest Territories; and

(b) to the legislature and government of each province in respect of all matters within the authority of the legislature of each province.

(2) Nothwithstanding subsection (1), section 15 shall not have effect until three years after this section comes into force.

33. (1) Parliament or the legislature of a province may expressly declare in an Act of Parliament or of the legislature, as the case may be, that the Act or a provision thereof shall operate notwithstanding a provision included in section 2 or sections 7 to 15 of this Charter.

(2) An Act or a provision of an Act in respect of which a declaration made under this section is in effect shall have such operation as it would have but for the provision of this Charter referred to in the declaration.

(3) A declaration made under subsection (1) shall cease to have effect five years after it comes into force or on such earlier date as may be specified in the declaration.

(4) Parliament or the legislature of a province may re–enact a declaration made under subsection (1).

(5) Subsection (3) applies in respect of a re–enactment made under subsection (4).

Citation

34. This Part may be cited as the Canadian Charter of Rights and Freedoms.

Part II

Rights of the Aboriginal Peoples of Canada

35. (1) The existing aboriginal and treaty rights of the aboriginal peoples of Canada are hereby recognized and affirmed.

(2) In this Act, "aboriginal peoples of Canada" includes the Indian, Inuit and Métis peoples of Canada.

Part III

Equalization and Regional Disparities

36. (1) Without altering the legislative authority of Parliament or of the Provincial legislatures, or the rights of any of them with

respect to the exercise of their legislative authority, Parliament and the legislatures, together with the government of Canada and the provincial governments, are committed to

(a) promoting equal opportunities for the well-being of Canadians;

(b) furthering economic development to reduce disparity in opportunities; and

(c) providing essential public services of reasonable quality to all Canadians.

(2) Parliament and the government of Canada are committed to the principle of making equalization payments to ensure that provincial governments have sufficient revenues to provide reasonably comparable levels of public services at reasonably comparable levels of taxation.

Part IV

Constitutional Conference

37. (1) A constitutional conference composed of the Prime Minister of Canada and the first ministers of the provinces shall be convened by the Prime Minister of Canada within one year after this Part comes into force.

(2) The conference convened under subsection (1) shall have included in its agenda an item respecting constitutional matters that directly affect the aboriginal peoples of Canada, including the identification and definition of the rights of those peoples to be included in the Constitution of Canada, and the Prime Minister of Canada shall invite representatives of those peoples to participate in the discussions on that item.

(3) The Prime Minister of Canada shall invite elected representatives of the governments of the Yukon Territory and the Northwest Territories to participate in the discussions on any item on the agenda of the conference convened under subsection (1) that, in the opinion of the Prime Minister, directly affects the Yukon Territory and the Northwest Territories.

Part V

Procedure for Amending Constitution of Canada

38. (1) An amendment to the Constitution of Canada may be made by proclamation issued by the Governor General under the Great Seal of Canada where so authorized by

(a) resolutions of the Senate and House of Commons; and

(b) resolutions of the legislative assemblies of at least two–thirds of the provinces that have, in the aggregate, according to the then latest general census, at least fifty per cent of the population of all the provinces.

(2) An amendment made under subsection (1) that derogates from the legislative powers, the proprietary rights or any other rights or privileges of the legislature or government of a province shall require a resolution supported by a majority of the members of each of the Senate, the House of Commons and the legislative assemblies required under subsection (1).

(3) An amendment referred to in subsection (2) shall not have effect in a province the legislative assembly of which has expressed its dissent thereto by resolution supported by a majority of its members prior to the issue of the proclamation to which the amendment relates unless that legislative assembly, subsequently, by resolution supported by a majority of its members, revokes its dissent and authorizes the amendment.

(4) A resolution of dissent made for the purposes of subsection (3) may be revoked at any time before or after the issue of the proclamation to which it relates.

39. (1) A proclamation shall not be issued under subsection 38(1) before the expiration of one year from the adoption of the resolution initiating the amendment procedure thereunder, unless the legislative assembly of each province has previously adopted a resolution of assent or dissent.

(2) A proclamation shall not be issued under subsection 38(1) after the expiration of three years from the adoption of the resolution initiating the amendment procedure thereunder.

40. Where an amendment is made under subsection 38(1) that transfers provincial legislative powers relating to education or other cultural matters from provincial legislatures to Parliament, Canada shall provide reasonable compensation to any province to which the amendment does not apply.

41. An amendment to the Constitution of Canada in relation to the following matters may be made by proclamation issued by the Governor General under the Great Seal of Canada only where authorized by resolutions of the Senate and House of Commons and of the legislative assembly of each province:

(a) the office of the Queen, the Governor General and the Lieutenant Governor of a province;

(b) the right of a province to a number of members in the House of Commons not less than the number of Senators by which the province is entitled to be represented at the time this Part comes into force;

(c) subject to section 43, the use of the English or the French language;

(d) the composition of the Supreme Court of Canada; and

(e) an amendment to this Part.

42. (1) An amendment to the Constitution of Canada in relation to the following matters may be made only in accordance with subsection 38(1):

(a) the principle of proportionate representation of the provinces in the House of Commons prescribed by the Constitution of Canada;

(b) the powers of the Senate and the method of selecting Senators;

(c) the number of members by which a province is entitled to be represented in the Senate and the residence qualifications of Senators;

(d) subject to paragraph 41(d), the Supreme Court of Canada;

(e) the extension of existing provinces into the territories; and

(f) notwithstanding any other law or practice, the establishment of new provinces.

(2) Subsections 38(2) to (4) do not apply in respect of amendments in relation to matters referred to in subsection (1).

43. An amendment to the Constitution of Canada, in relation to any provision that applies to one or more, but not all, provinces, including

(a) any alteration to boundaries between provinces, and

(b) any amendment to any provision that relates to the use of the English or the French language within a province,

may be made by proclamation issued by the Governor General under the Great Seal of Canada only where so authorized by resolutions of the Senate and House of Commons and of the legislative assembly of each province to which the amendment applies.

44. Subject to sections 41 and 42, Parliament may exclusively make laws amending the Constitution of Canada in relation to the executive government of Canada or the Senate and House of Commons.

45. Subject to section 41, the legislature of each province may exclusively make laws amending the constitution of the province.

46. (1) The procedures for amendment under sections 38, 41, 42 and 43 may be initiated either by the Senate or the House of Commons or by the legislative assembly of a province.

(2) A resolution of assent made for the purposes of this Part may be revoked at any time before the issue of a proclamation authorized by it.

47. (1) An amendment to the Constitution of Canada made by proclamation under section 38, 41, 42 or 43 may be made without a resolution of the Senate authorizing the issue of the proclamation if, within one hundred and eighty days after the adoption by the House of Commons of a resolution authorizing its issue, the Senate has not adopted such a resolution and if, at any time after the expiration of that period, the House of Commons again adopts the resolution.

(2) Any period when Parliament is prorogued or dissolved shall not be counted in computing the one hundred and eighty day period referred to in subsection (1).

48. The Queen's Privy Council for Canada shall advise the Governor General to issue a proclamation under this Part forthwith on the adoption of the resolutions required for an amendment made by proclamation under this Part.

49. A constitutional conference composed of the Prime Minister of Canada and the first ministers of the provinces shall be convened by the Prime Minister of Canada within fifteen years after this Part comes into force to review the provisions of this Part.

Part VI

Amendment to the Constitution Act, 1867

50. The Constitution Act, 1867 (formerly named the British North America Act, 1867) is amended by adding thereto, immediately after section 92 thereof, the following heading and section:

"Non–Renewable Natural Resources, Forestry Resources and Electrical Energy

92A. (1) In each province, the legislature may exlusively make laws in relation to

(a) exploration for non–renewable natural resources in the province;

(b) development, conservation and management of non–renewable natural resources and forestry resources in the province, including laws in relation to the rate of primary production therefrom; and

(c) development, conservation and management of sites and facilities in the province for the generation and production of electrical energy.

(2) In each province, the lgislature may make laws in relation to the export from the province to another part of Canada of the primary production from non-renewable natural resources and forestry resources in the province and the production from facilities in the province for the generation of electrical energy, but such laws may not authorize or provide for discrimination in prices or in supplies exported to another part of Canada.

(3) Nothing in subsection (2) derogates from the authority of Parliament to enact laws in relation to the matters referred to in that subsection and, where such a law of Parliament and a law of a province conflict, the law of Parliament prevails to the extent of the conflict.

(4) In each province, the legislature may make laws in relation to the raising of money by any mode or system of taxation in respect of

(a) non-renewable natural resources and forestry resources in the province and the primary production therefrom, and

(b) sites and facilities in the province for the generation of electrical energy and the production therefrom,

whether or not such production is exported in whole or in part from the province, but such laws may not authorize or provide for taxation that differentiates between production exported to another part of Canada and production not exported from the province.

(5) The expression "primary production" has the meaning assigned by the Sixth Schedule.

(6) Nothing in subsections (1) to (5) derogates from any powers or rights that a legislature or government of a province had immediately before the coming into force of this section."

51. The said Act is further amended by adding thereto the following Schedule:

"The Sixth Schedule

Primary Production from Non-Renewable Natural Resources and Forestry Resources

1. For the purposes of section 92A of this Act,
(a) production from a non-renewable natural resource is primarily production therefrom if
(i) it is in the form in which it exists upon its recovery or severance from its natural state, or
(ii) it is a product resulting from processing or refining the resource, and is not a manufactured product or a product resulting from refining crude oil, refining upgraded heavy crude oil, refining gases or liquids derived from coal or refining a synthetic equivalent of crude oil; and
(b) production from a forestry resource is primary production therefrom if it consists of sawlogs, poles, lumber, wood chips, sawdust or any other primary wood product, or wood pulp, and is not a product manufactured from wood."

PART VII

General

52. (1) The Constitution of Canada is the supreme law of Canada, and any law that is inconsistent with the provisions of the Constitution is, to the extent of the inconsistency, of no force or effect.

(2) The Constitution of Canada includes
(a) the Canada Act 1982, including this Act;
(b) the Acts and orders referred to in the schedule; and
(c) any amendment to any Act or order referred to in paragraph (a) or (b).

(3) Amendments to the Constitution of Canada shall be made only in accordance with the authority contained in the Constitution of Canada.

53. (1) The enactments referred to in Column I of the schedule are hereby repealed or amended to the extent indicated in Column II thereof and, unless repealed, shall continue as law in Canada under the names set out in Column III thereof.

(2) Every enactment, except the Canada Act 1982, that refers to an enactment referred to in the schedule by the name in Column I thereof is hereby amended by substituting for that name the corresponding name in Column III thereof, and any British North America Act not referred to in the schedule may be cited as the Constitution Act followed by the year and number, if any, of its enactment.

54. Part IV is repealed on the day that is one year after this Part comes into force and this section may be repealed and this Act renumbered, consequentially upon the repeal of Part IV and this section, by proclamation issued by the Governor General under the Great Seal of Canada.

55. A French version of the portions of the Constitution of Canada referred to in the schedule shall be prepared by the Minister of Justice of Canada as expeditiously as possible and, when any portion thereof sufficient to warrant action being taken has been so prepared, it shall be put forward for enactment by proclamation issued by the Governor General under the Great Seal of Canada pursuant to the procedure then applicable to an amendment of the same provisions of the Constitution of Canada.

56. Where any portion of the Constitution of Canada has been or is enacted in English and French or where a French version of any portion of the Constitution is enacted pursuant to section 55, the English and French versions of that portion of the Constitution are equally authoritative.

57. The English and French versions of this Act are equally authoritative.

58. Subject to section 59, this Act shall come into force on a day to be fixed by proclamation issued by the Queen or the Governor General under the Great Seal of Canada.

59. (1) Paragraph 23(1)(a) shall come into force in respect of Quebec on a day to be fixed by proclamation issued by the Queen or the Governor General under the Great Seal of Canada.

(2) A proclamation under subsection (1) shall be issued only where authorized by the legislative assembly or government of Quebec.

(3) This section may be repealed on the day paragraph 23(1)(a) comes into force in respect of Quebec and this Act amended and renumbered, consequentially upon the repeal of this section, by proclamation issued by the Queen or the Governor General under the Great Seal of Canada.

60. This Act may be cited as the Constitution Act, 1982, and the Constitution Acts 1867 to 1975 (No. 2) and this Act may be cited together as the Constitution Acts, 1867 to 1982.

Index